He Inclined His Ear unto Me

W. Stephen Keel

Because we serve a triune God this book has three titles...

Escape from Christianity
He Inclined His Ear unto Me
The Devine Chorography

W. Stephen Keel

BIBLE transMISSION

2015

HE INCLINED HIS EAR UNTO ME by W. Stephen Keel

Published by Bible TransMission
3900 Milton Highway
Ringgold, VA 24586
www.bibletransmission.org

Follow us: https://www.facebook.com/bibletransmission and
https://twitter.com/bibletrans

This book or parts thereof may not be reproduced in any form, stored in a retrieval system, or transmitted in any form by any means, electronic, mechanical, photocopy, recorded, or otherwise, without prior written permission of the publisher except as provided by United States of America copyright law.

Scripture taken from the New King James Version®. Copyright © 1982 by Thomas Nelson. Used by permission. All rights reserved.

THE HOLY BIBLE, NEW INTERNATIONAL VERSION®, NIV® Copyright © 1973, 1978, 1984, 2011 by Biblica, Inc.® Used by permission. All rights reserved worldwide.

Copyright © 2015 by Bible TransMission

All rights reserved.

Cover design © 2015 by Nancy S. Keeler

Photograph © 1982 by Nancy H. Keel

Visit the author's website at www.bibletransmission.org.

Library of Congress Control Number: 2015935577

International Standard Book Number: ISBN-10: 0692398023
ISBN-13: 978-0-692-39802-9

Printed in the United States of America

I love the LORD, because He hears My voice *and* my supplications. Because He has inclined His ear to me, Therefore I shall call *upon Him* as long as I live.

Psalm 116:1-2

I will bless the LORD at all times;
His praise *shall* continually *be* in my mouth.
My soul shall make its boast in the LORD;
The humble shall hear *of it* and be glad.
Oh, magnify the LORD with me,
And let us exalt His name together.
I sought the LORD, and He heard me,
And delivered me from all my fears.
They looked to Him and were radiant,
And their faces were not ashamed.
This poor man cried out, and the LORD heard *him,*
And saved him out of all his troubles.
The angel of the LORD encamps all around those who fear Him,
And delivers them.

Psalm 34:1-7

Table of Contents

W. Stephen Keel

Foreword i
Introduction: Mundane or Marvelous? 1
Chapter 1: He Inclined His Ear unto Me 7
    Major Miracles and Minor Miracles 9
    Embracing Absurdity 13
Chapter 2: Wives First 20
Chapter 3: From the World of Darkness into the Light 28
    Topsy Turvy – My World Flip Flops 37
    Baby Steps in Jesus 43
    To Be a Preacher or Not to Be a Preacher 46
Chapter 4: Escape from Christianity 51
    Escape from Christianity Continued 53
    The Calling of a Spiritual Mid-wife 55
    Hold My Tongue, O God 59
Chapter 5: I Talk, He Listens, Things Happen 65
    Man Plans, But God Executes 70
    Hearing My Name at the Office Supply Store 72
Chapter 6: Hearing Can Be About Hearing 76
    The Lord Gives Better than He Takes 79
Chapter 7: Is this it, or is there something else? 85
Chapter 8: Headaches 94
    More Healings 97
Chapter 9: A Miracle among the Maggots 103
    Oh, go on… (An Expression of Polite Disbelief) 105
    I Am Worth More Dead than Alive, Not… 108
Chapter 10: Royal Priests 115
Chapter 11: For What Purpose? 125
Chapter 12: The Abnormal Can Be Normal 130

He Inclined His Ear

Chapter 13: The Divine Choreography 135
Chapter 14: Addendum 150
Chapter 15: Other Stories 157
   August 2010: A Real Challenge 157
   March 2011: Another day in the life of Steve aka Dad Keel. 159
   November 2011: Stephen Keel - New Lung Needed - Monday 11/28 Update 161
   October 2012: Plans for Steve's Celebration 165
Epilogue 167
   The End of the Beginning 170
   Be Strong and Courageous 173
Life in Pictures 177

W. Stephen Keel

Foreword

The lights shimmered brightly off of the thin blanket of snow and the rolls of razor sharp barbed wire. The icy chill hanging in the air was making my nose and ears numb but I was not thinking much of it. The year was 1994 and I was standing in the parking lot of Caswell Correctional Center just outside of Yanceyville, North Carolina. I looked up nervously at my Dad in hope of gaining a little more confidence not knowing exactly what was in store. Two guards approached the gate surrounded by steel fence.

"Evening, Steve." The first one muttered. "Sure is cold out." I saw his eyes shift over to me and his face changed to a look of obvious disapproval.

"Who you got with you tonight?"

"This is my son, Zeke." Dad responded.

"You got permission?" The guard asked?

"Yes." Dad said.

"Ok well let's go then."

A loud buzzer sounded, the gate rolled open, and we were ushered into a heavily fortified cinderblock guard shack. The room was physically clean and warm yet still felt cold and sterile. I looked around the room and saw steel doors with heavy locks, wired safety glass, and security cameras hanging in the corners. A woman who sat at a desk behind a walled and glass partition pushed a clip board through a slot for us to sign in.

Again courtesies were exchanged and again the woman at the desk locked on to me with the same look of disapproval I had seemed moments before.

"How old are you son?" She asked.

"I'm 14," I sheepishly replied.

He Inclined His Ear

Dad reassured her that we had the warden's permission, but she still grabbed her radio and made a call. A few moments later, she gave a nod and guards proceeded to search us. We removed our coats, and they were emptied. We were patted down, wallets were opened, Dad's Bible was opened and flipped between pages, and his old guitar and case was carefully inspected inside and out.

Once they completed the inspection, a guard took us to the last heavy steel plated door between us and the main compound. The guard gave me a final stern instruction to follow him and stay on the sidewalk. I was sure I had no intentions of leaving his side anyway. I kept glancing in curiosity at the large pistol that hung off his hip. Another loud buzzer sounded and the door swung open bringing another cold blast of air in with it.

We stepped out into the compound. It was surprisingly quiet. No inmates were visible. All I could see were a series of buildings connected by sidewalks and what looked like a basketball court off at the far end. The guard escorted us to the one of the buildings. We entered the single room structure and I found it to be very plain. There were no wall decorations or carpet. Just four block walls, a hard laminate floor, and a few folding chairs and a folding table over in a corner. A clock hung on the wall just over the door. The only unique item was an easel with large squares of paper on it.

Dad and I grabbed a couple of chairs and took a seat. After a mostly quite uncomfortable ten minute wait, the clock struck seven and moments later the door opened. A group of maybe 15 inmates in uniform shuffled their way into the room, most with Bibles in hand, followed by several more armed guards. In this particular group each individual had requested to attend so everyone was there on their own accord. They were men of all ages, and races. Some had shackles between their legs and others were allowed to walk freely. They stayed in line to get their chairs from the stack and then assembled them in a semi-circle around the easel.

As the men settled in, they all greeted one another with real warmth and care for one another. Dad quickly introduced me to the group, and although I was leery of everyone there, I was met with smiles and feelings of acceptance. The guards took positions around the door and seemed to give general freedom for everyone to move inside the room. After maybe five minutes of greetings everyone took a seat. Dad asked for one of the inmates to open us up with prayer and he obliged.

After the short prayer, Dad picked up his old classical six string guitar and played a couple of worship songs in the key of C. I am pretty sure this was the only key he ever learned to play in but he got pretty good at it. As the men sang, I could feel a calm settle over the room. Some men sang passionately, while others remained silent but engaged. The clock on the wall kept spinning towards 7:55 p.m. when the men were scheduled to leave, but I could sense that time, the guards, and the fences no longer gripped the room as tightly.

By age 14, I had heard my Dad give perhaps hundreds of sermons. He was the personality that genuinely enjoyed getting in front of any available audience and could speak comfortably for hours even at an impromptu event. Once the singing had ended, I expected Dad to take over and go right into what he liked to do best. Instead, he nodded to one of the inmates, a very skinny middle aged man with tattoos down his arm and around his neck.

I could sense the man was nervous. He stepped forward to the easel, pulled out his Bible and a single sheet of paper which were his notes and he began. His sermon was from 1 Corinthians 13, about love.

In all honesty it was pretty rough, but it came from the heart. I had memorized this particular chapter in its entirety years before and even at my young age had heard more sermons based around it than I could recount. I was pretty sure I had heard all the analogies and examples you could make off this passage. Now when it was delivered by a convict who had been banished from society, locked in a cage, and forgotten for years to come, the message changed. Yet it remained the same.

All of the men followed along in their Bibles and listened intently. I could sense his confidence growing as he spoke and the men responded to the message. When he finished, the men discussed openly giving opinions and asking questions about what they had just covered. They then took the remaining minutes to share anything they wanted

He Inclined His Ear

to and then pray with and for each other. The moments were real and you could see the men being touched.

When the clock hit the 55 minute, one of the guards called for us to wrap it up. The inmates all folded their chairs and put them back in the stack against the wall and fell back in line. The guard opened the door and with an icy blast, the prison resumed to its original form. The men shuffled out the door in the same manner in which they entered. One guard stayed behind, and after waiting several minutes, he escorted us back out across the compound to the guard shack.

In my youth I never really processed exactly what my Dad took me to see. He had been going to meet with these men for years and he continued to do so for many more. In hindsight, it wasn't just about what I saw, but also what I did not see.

We never met a greeter or an usher. We never saw a hymnal or heard a band play. Who knows how far you might have had to drive to find an ordained minister. Yet for even all the things that were not there, where Dad had taken me was actually quite simple. He had just taken me to church.

That night from my youth was merely a snapshot into a defining portion of my Dad's journey. This one night was my last due to a change of heart, perhaps due to complaints to the warden, as I was no longer allowed back. His involvement with prison ministry I believe shaped many of his views into the shortcomings to the modern church which all who knew him came to learn. I believe it was in this seemingly hopeless and empty setting where he found the virtues of simplicity and real participation that created a deeper experience when all the distractions were removed. He had moments he told me of sitting in the hall of solitary confinement in which the inmates would curse him, spit at him, and even throw feces at him. In these dark situations filled with men of the lowest denomination, he would describe through worship finding a peace that would fill the room and calm even the darkest hearts.

Steve Keel was a driven man. Once he set to a task, no matter the size, he rarely failed to complete it. Just as this church he took me to seems unorthodox, so Dad was somewhat unorthodox in his life and his relationship with God. He had a remarkable spiritual journey that I

W. Stephen Keel

think can be similarly paralleled to one of his favorite works, *Pilgrim's Progress*. His journey was hard, and the path was narrow with many distractions, challenges, and stumbling blocks, but he stayed the course. This book is about his life and walk with God from his experience and perspective. He was at times not fully accepted by his peers, I think largely due to his sometimes intimidating presence and ability to speak out and say what others would not. Those who were able to see him eye-to-eye and engage with his drive and vision would all tell you he was a man of great energy and passion who will not be soon forgotten.

He lived a life as a high school football star, fisherman, marksman, outdoorsman, bush pilot, teacher, farrier, print shop operator, entrepreneur, inventor of multiple patented items, expert in wind speed measurement, construction manager, computer networking and equipment specialist, salesman, businessman, and so much more, all in the course of raising seven children. Yet even in all these things he engaged in, he lived ultimately to please and to serve Christ. On many occasions he would challenge me but also many others as to what are you doing to share the love of God? He lived the message that in giving of oneself that is where one can receive the blessing. As Jesus challenged Peter in John 21:15 and beyond, "if you love me, feed my sheep."

I hope as you read this book you will find something new. Perhaps an insight into your own spirituality, encouragement, instruction, an insight into yourself, or an insight into Steve Keel, you may not have known for those who knew him and may or may not have fully understood him. Because of his dynamic personality and extraordinary journey I believe you will find something here for you. I am confident that his desire in this book is that whatever morsel you take away might be a seed planted for the glory of God.

Ezekiel (Zeke) Keel

He Inclined His Ear

W. Stephen Keel

Introduction: Mundane or Marvelous?

I'd like to invite you into my dining room several years ago. My wife was working diligently to reconcile our checkbook. The house was full of the sounds of our many children, and I was playing with them as she worked. She worked a long time. She was stuck in a place where she needed to locate a $200 amount to reconcile our check book with the bank's records, but she could not find it.

With a confident attitude of male superiority, I told her that she obviously needed my help. "I can fix this in a short period of time."

She had worked for 2 hours, reviewing several months of statements. Because I was the "macho man", the computer sales person with excellent math skills, I knew I could solve it in a few minutes. God had a different plan. I puzzled over the problem for more than an hour. No matter how I added up the numbers or evaluated the debits and credits, I could not solve the problem.

Finally I did what I should have done in the first place. I prayed. I closed my eyes and held my wife's hand and said, "Father, in the name of Jesus, I apologize for my attitude toward my wife. My ego has gotten in the way of my ability to solve this problem. I know that You resist the proud. I humble myself before You, and I am declaring that I cannot on my own solve this problem. I ask You, in the name of Jesus, to show me where the mistake is that's causing the problem. Thank You, Lord, for Your goodness, in the name of Jesus, Amen."

I opened my eyes and looked at the paper by my left hand. My eyes fell on a column of numbers. There in plain sight was the $200 amount that had prevented the reconciliation. It was a rent check for my daughter who was attending the University of Virginia. I exclaimed excitedly, "Praise the Lord! There is the answer right there!"

As soon as I said that, my son Ezekiel said to me, "Gee, Dad, why didn't you pray sooner?" That is the quintessential question: why don't we pray sooner? Why don't we invite God into our mess, our circumstances, and our difficulties? Now, it is not as if I hadn't had experiences that would have taught me this. I had!

He Inclined His Ear

A number of years previously, we had been living in New Mexico. We had visited Carlsbad Caverns in the southern part of the state. It's a deep hole in the ground. Our family walked through the bat infested entrance of the cave. We passed the stalactites and stalagmites along the several miles of paths. We rested occasionally because my wife was pregnant and the younger children needed rest.

Near the end of the trail, we realized that little Charissa had lost the hat that matched her very expensive Rothschild plaid wool coat from England. This coat had been a special gift from a friend. We were quite distressed to see that she didn't have her hat. We looked for a park ranger to ask him how we could try to find it. It had been lost a mile behind us, and neither my wife nor I had the time or strength to back-track and look for it. Charissa may have dropped it into a pool or over an embankment. The situation looked bleak.

We prayed, "Father, thank You for this hat and coat. Thank You for our sister in the Lord who was so kind to us to give us this little coat and hat. We are deep down in the bowels of the earth. There's no reasonable way that we can expect to find this hat. We can only trust in You. We ask You Lord, in the name of Jesus to show us where this hat is. We opened our eyes and saw a park ranger walking toward us from the direction opposite from the way we had come. In his hand he had the hat! Looking at little Charissa's coat, he said to us, "Is this your hat?"

Alleluia! Of course it was.

We learned that there were two trails, a long one and a short one. We had walked on the long one, and the ranger had walked on the short one. This explained why we met him coming toward us from the opposite direction. Not only had he found the hat, but he had delivered it to us at the precise moment that we prayed. For us, it was a miracle. It was a wonderful miracle!

Recently, I was working on a computer for Lancy Levielle, the Creole voice and translator for my radio program "A Proverb a Day" in Haiti. The project involved taking a two hard drives from a failed computer and installing them in an identical replacement computer. I struggled for two hours and could not get the replacement computer to work.

W. Stephen Keel

In my frustration, I closed my eyes and I said, "Lord, I don't understand it. Please, in the name of Jesus, help me understand this problem so that I can resolve it."

I opened my eyes, and I saw that the computer that I was working on had three hard drives in it. All along I had been working under the assumption that there were two hard drives. One of the hard drives was in a hidden location, and I had mistaken it for another piece of equipment. As soon as I identified the third drive, I was able to fix the computer. In my spirit, I felt that I had solved the problem too late. I had not prayed soon enough, but it reinforced the idea that I need to pray sooner next time. Those hours had been wasted.

In spite of these experiences, I was not very good at praying at the "first" beginning. I hope that after reading this book, you will be better than I was at asking the Lord to intervene in the details of your life. This book is written about everyday life experiences. It is written about walking in the spirit as a normal human being.

I am of the opinion that many people are missing out on the excitement of having an ongoing conversation with Jesus. They are living lives that are unnecessarily mundane. They are being careful to control their tongues and to watch out for their children's safety. They are attending church meetings regularly and participating in related events, but many find themselves underfed and under-satisfied. Here is an important question...

"When was the last time you heard the voice of the Lord....when was the last time you cried out to God, and He answered you in a clear way where there is no question in your mind that God answered your prayer?"

Talking to the Lord and having Him talk to us are central, essential elements of the Christian life. In John chapter 10, Jesus states very clearly, "My sheep hear My voice."

He also says, "I am the good Shepherd."

We know from Psalm 23 that "He leads in paths of righteousness for His name sake and that His rod and staff comfort us. He makes us rest in green pastures." For many Christians, it is difficult to export these concepts from the Sunday school discussions into everyday life.

He Inclined His Ear

I hope to be an inspiration to Christians who are living mundane lives. I also want to be a challenge to people who have rejected the concept that God wants to literally walk and talk with His children.

I have a good friend who grew up in the Mormon Church. He made a decision as a child to become a Mormon of Mormons. He greatly respected the church. At an early age he gave himself over to the study of the doctrines of the church. One of the most important concepts of the Mormon Church is the role of the family in the believer's life, including the believer's future position in heaven.

My friend was eager to fulfill everything that was possible for himself, his wife and his children. Not long after his third child had been born, he came home to discover that his wife had left him. He had no previous discussions with her about leaving, and he had no idea that this was going to happen.

The divorce was a tremendous blow to him. It challenged his core understanding of his relationship with God. "If I am working so hard to please You, God, how could You allow something of this nature to happen to me?"

The blow was so severe that he was thrown into a state of confusion and became suicidal. He tried to take his life on more than one occasion. He spent several months in the hospital following an automobile accident that was a suicide attempt. After months in full body traction where he was unable to move or fight his circumstances, he found an inner sense of submission to his circumstances. He began to embrace the idea of continuing to live. Unlike many who found a close connection to God in situations like this, he became determined to live in total rejection of God, the Bible and religion. He worked hard to divorce himself from the realm wherein he had suffered such profound hurt.

I developed a relationship with this man because I saw and continue to see in him spiritual deposits from the hand of God that mold his character and personality. In spite of his rejection of God, I really like the guy. I like him well enough to spend time with him and continue to cultivate friendship.

W. Stephen Keel

Often, I make mention of the fact that I prayed or I am going to pray or I have had an answer to prayer. My friend is totally comfortable telling me that I am completely crazy to bother with such ideas as praying and asking God for help. I often desire to show him the other side of the story. On a particular day, I had what appeared to be an opportunity.

My friend was setting up a computer system for a business he was operating. In response to his graciousness toward me, I had determined that I would help him set up his computers. I worked diligently at it. There was software we were attempting to install that simply would not work.

Here I was again; another black hole in cyberspace. Because I had worked as a computer professional, I knew enough to ask for help. I spent approximately two hours on the telephone with the technical support people from the company that had written the software. By lunchtime, we were still unable to make the software work.

We went to lunch and sat at a table. I said, "I think the problem here is that I haven't prayed about it."

He said, "That's ridiculous! Praying about it won't make any difference."

I said, "No, I have had these experiences where I could not get anything done. Then I asked God for help, and He gave me help. So here's what we are going to do: I am going to pray and ask God to help me, and I am going to believe that when we go back to work on this problem again, the problem will be solved in just a few minutes after we get back. Today you will see an answer to prayer."

We prayed, "Father, in the name of Jesus, here is a problem that I can't solve. You not only know how the universe is put together, You know how this computer is put together and how the software runs. In You dwells all wisdom and knowledge.

"You even know the people who are trying to help me out. As I humble myself before You, please, in the name of Jesus, give me the solution to this problem. I thank You for it in advance. I thank You that we are going to see this prayer answered....in the name of Jesus, Amen."

He Inclined His Ear

We went back to the office. The first thing I did was call the software company.

As it happened, perchance, the man that answered the phone was different from the one that I was talking to before. I described the problem to him, and he said, "The solution is such and such."

I acted on the simple instructions he provided and the problem was fixed. What we hadn't been able to solve in two hours previously was solved in two minutes.

This leads us to another problem; there were ten lepers and Jesus healed them all, but only one of them returned to give God thanks. Jesus asked, "Where are the other nine?" Unfortunately, it's not enough to see the hand of God move to convert a man to serve the Lord. Although my friend was conscious of what happened, it did not overcome the discouragement in his life and his reasons for rejecting Christianity; but, just maybe; it turned him a little bit in the right direction. As it turns out, he barely remembers the incident.

Many Christians are eager to see the hand of God move. Even though this is a book about the evidence of the hand of God moving in my life, I know that there is a much higher calling and a much greater need. That greater need is that we behold the face of God. As we behold the face of God, we are changed from glory to glory. Furthermore, if you are focused on the face of God, the presence of Jesus, and the character of God; then you also have the hand of God. My good friend Arthur Burt has said many times, "The greater includes the lesser, but the lesser does not necessarily include the greater."

What is a miracle for one man standing in the presence of God is merely a coincidence for another man. It's my hope that these testimonies, that you are about to read, will not be considered chance or limit you from seeing the hand of God in unbelief. I am hoping that you will be provoked to seek the face of God.

W. Stephen Keel

Chapter 1: He Inclined His Ear unto Me

I love the Lord, because he hath heard my voice. He inclined his ear unto me. Therefore will I call upon him, while I live. Psalm 16:1

What a controversial statement. Throughout history, men have snickered at the probability that the man that says that he hears the voice of God is a religious nut. Is it possible that the God of the universe would incline His ear unto mere man? How could dirt and hydrogen mixed in a cosmic soup and baked in a cosmic oven until it composed great musical symphonies be of any personal interest to a non-existent God. If by grace we overcome this hurdle and actually believe in God then, what is the likelihood that this God would actually talk to or listen to you or me specifically rather than in some sort of liturgical generic sense?

Is it not reasonable that this concept of talking to God is a left-over from Greek mythology where the gods and goddesses had human wants and weaknesses, carrying on soap-opera like relationships with men?

I have struggled to bring this book into existence. There is a great danger that it is not spiritually kosher, because it is written in the first person. My children often tell me that my favorite subject is myself. Although we joke about it, it cuts my heart that I might risk drawing attention to me when Jesus is the main event. So I apologize for writing in the first person. Great men of God have overcome this problem by writing anonymously. My meager explanation for writing in the first person is two-fold:

1. The man that was blind from birth told his story in the first person. He said that he could not explain or answer the questions that were being posed to him by the Pharisees, and he said, "I do not know the answer to your questions, but this I do know. I was blind and now I see."

2. I believe the Lord has told me to write in the first person.

He Inclined His Ear

From a theological perspective, the central issue surrounding the stories in this book has been framed around two competing concepts; theism and deism. A deist, like Thomas Jefferson, believes that there is a god. He did, in fact, set the world in order according to immutable laws that are identifiable and observable. After He created things, He perched Himself on a limb of a tree far off in a complex universe to occasionally and whimsically peer into the affairs of men through a pair of cosmic binoculars. He is out there more or less observing His handiwork.

Au contraire, the theist similarly acknowledges the hand of the Creator. Today He is being referred to as the "Intelligent Designer." But the theist, like David, knows that God inclines His ear unto him, and that not only does He incline His ear, but He actually answers prayer in direct and specific ways.

You might say that I am preaching to the choir. I think not. Most evangelical Christians will tell you that they are theistic, but in reality, they are deistic. This is proven by the fact that they do not diligently seek Him. The Scripture is clear. Without faith, it is impossible to please God. According to the writer of Hebrews, you have to believe that He is and that He is the Rewarder of those who diligently seek Him. Many people believe that He is, but do they believe that He is the Rewarder of those that diligently seek Him?

That question can be answered, not by filling out forms with multiple choice questions on a Sunday school class personality test, but by simply looking at one's attitudes and actions. Is the self-defined theist diligently seeking Him? If he is, that is a good sign that he believes that He is the Rewarder of those that diligently seek Him. If he isn't, then it is likely that he is living a lie.

It seems that history has a way of alternately admiring and ridiculing people who claim to hear the voice of God. I saw a bumper sticker recently that said, "Even though the voices in my head are not real, they have some great ideas."

If the right people had asked Joan of Arc about her visions, insights and directions from God, they would have locked her up, instead of releasing her to the battle field. I have met men in prisons who are attempting to convince others that they have heard God speak. Many

W. Stephen Keel

times they are unsuccessful because their character and actions don't represent the kind of life that should appear in a person who is hearing from God.

Perhaps the most prevalent reason for ignoring the voice of God is the idea that those things that appear to happen as the result of God speaking to a man are mere coincidence. Chaos theory tells us how reasonable it is, in a universe billions of years old, that I can drive down the road in an automobile recording my voice digitally. This is reasonable simply because we have had enough time for this sort of thing to randomly occur.

One of the purposes of this volume is to dispel this myth. Even after you have heard or read two or three of these testimonies, you might still say, "Well, that is an example of pure coincidence." It is my hope that after you have heard 20, 30, or 40 "coincidences", you may begin to agree that God does incline His ear to the voice of man.

This is my hope and my reason for setting these things forth. This isn't a treatise on miracles, but it does include the subject of the supernatural. I could refer to these things as "mystical," but that would identify me with people who are considered to be "special." I am just a dad, a sometimes businessman, and a sometimes worker in the kingdom of heaven.

I am not a pastor with a congregation or a religious professional using my experiences with God to raise money. I say unkind things to my wife and succeed in alienating my children with unsuccessful attempts to walk as a Godly father figure. I have been free from debt, but I also know what it is like to have more bills than I could possibly pay in the foreseeable future. I am not "any man." I am me and you are you. You can hear God's voice too. Try it. You will like it.

Major Miracles and Minor Miracles

Some people categorize major miracles and minor miracles. I am going to mention a couple of minor miracles that have major implications.

Early in my Christian experience, I was given insight into verses in Proverbs chapter 3. The scripture teaches clearly:

He Inclined His Ear

"Trust in the Lord with all thine heart and lean not on thy own understanding. In all thy ways acknowledge Him, and He shall direct thy path."

I discovered that acknowledging Him was simply a matter of being conscious, on a moment by moment basis of the fact that the sovereign God of the universe was aware of me…that He has inclined His ear unto me and is actively involved in everything that is going on about me. He is executing a plan that has been conceived before the beginning of time. This is a high thought. It is made real by grace through faith.

The Lord has worked in my life to increase my faith. He did this, in part, by allowing me to question the amount of detail involved in His directing of my steps.

In 1986, I was working as a volunteer chaplain in a maximum custody prison in Blanch, North Carolina. The facility was a somewhat frightening anachronism. It is now an abandoned concrete, steel hulk. It had been built in the 1950's in the style of an ancient dungeon. It was very cold. It reminded me of a building built for the slaughter of animals. It housed 125 young men between the ages of 18 and 23. They were the best of the worst; that is, those that were very good at being bad. They had been culled from prisons around the state of North Carolina and had found their way to maximum custody at Blanch.

The building was set up in the shape of a "T," two stories high. When you entered the building you could go to the right and there were two stories of cells, or you could go to the left and there were two more stories of cells. Or, you could go straight ahead to the kitchen area downstairs. It had an area known as "segregation" upstairs. There was a small 4 cells, brick "hole" outside that was reserved for overachievers in the world of evil. The residents of the "hole" were special people that would not likely go to a service at the local Episcopal Church. In fact there was no "local" Episcopal Church as Blanch Prison was located in a remote corner of Caswell County far from stop lights and Starbucks.

My pattern of ministry was to go into the cell blocks and share the gospel in the hallway between the two rows of cells. One particular day, I was meditating on the Word of God. Does He in fact direct our steps, if we acknowledge Him? I was standing on the second floor near the centrally located guard room as I pondered this thought. I asked the Lord this question. "Lord, if You are really directing my steps, is there any way that it would make a difference whether I went down the stairs on the left side of the control room or went down the stairs on the right side of the control room?"

It was obvious to me that whether I went down one or the other, I would end up at the same place downstairs. "Does it really matter to You, Lord, which set of steps I use because I end up at the same place on first floor? I am going to acknowledge You and go down this set of stairs and hope to understand why You would even have me ask this question."

As I neared the bottom of the stairs, I met an inmate whom I knew fairly well, who was a trustee in the system. He had freedom to move about, unlike the others who were locked up in their individual maximum custody cells. He was storming up the steps with rage and anger on his face. I grabbed him by the arm and said, "Whoa, I don't know where you are going, but I know you are not in the right spirit. Come with me! You and I have got to have a talk."

I took him down the steps into a room where I frequently counseled the men. I said, "Okay, what's going on?"

He said, "I was on my way to murder a man. If you hadn't stopped me, he would be dead by now."

I said, "It was clear to me that you had something like that in mind. Let's talk about it." So, we talked about it and worked through the problem, and the man that he was going to murder is alive today, and I have this story to tell you about how I acknowledged God and He directed my steps.

I had a similar experience many years later. I was in Haiti. After a short walk, I became disoriented in a community that had no sign posts. There were foot paths among a sprawling array of huts and homes covering several square miles. I had been in the area five years earlier, and I knew where I wanted to go. I knew that if I could get to a certain spot, I could see a landmark to guide me. I could walk toward the landmark to get to where I intended to go. It was also

He Inclined His Ear

possible that I could turn aimlessly and not find anything. Because I could not speak Creole, I could not ask for directions. I wanted to avoid getting in a situation where I would not know how to get back to my host's home.

Once again I sought the Lord asking the "steps" question.

I said, "Lord, is there any likelihood that it matters when the road splits ahead which road I take? I can turn right and explore the land with hopes of being able to see a familiar landmark, or I can turn left and go back to where I came from and walk the two or three miles further than is necessary to get to my destination. So, Lord, does it really matter whether I turn to the left or to the right?"

Holding this thought I arrived at the "Y" in the path. I decided to take a risk, in faith, and go to the right into the area that was somewhat unknown.

God's grace prevailed and as I walked around a large building, I looked and saw the landmark I needed to give me my orientation. I proceeded a little further down the path, where I stepped onto what some call a road. It wasn't much of a road. Vehicles could use it only when weather was dry enough. Almost immediately I saw a yellow school bus filled with young Americans both in and on the bus. This was quite a surprise because the United Nations Peacekeepers were in Haiti and had circulated letters asking all Americans to leave for their own safety. We waved to each other and the bus stopped. A man got off the bus and approached me. He introduced himself saying he was a pastor from Florida bringing a group of kids on a mission trip. He asked me what I was doing in Les Cayes.

I told him that I had been broadcasting a radio program in that community for a number of years and that I was visiting to discover if there had been any value or impact from the programs. He said, "Well, you need to meet Pastor Luis. He lives 100 yards up the road. I think he is home right now, but I am sure that you need to meet him."

So I thanked the man and walked up the road to the dwelling he told me about. At the precise moment that I arrived at the gate, Pastor Luis was driving out of his driveway. I spoke to him, told him who I

W. Stephen Keel

was and asked if it was possible for us to get together. He said, "Come by this afternoon at four o'clock and we will chat. I have to go right now."

I went back at four o'clock. I had plenty of free time to visit him because my other purpose for being there was to speak at a conference. The conference was over, and now I had a couple of days of unscheduled time. I was out and about checking out the countryside and seeking a visit with some old friends.

My meeting with Pastor Luis resulted in three preaching events the following day, one of them was on regional TV and the other two were on national radio that included a feed into the Haitian community in southern Florida. At the end of the third preaching, Pastor Luis told me that the words he had heard had affected his entire ministry and the course of his life would be changed by what he heard.

Now this appears to have happened somewhat randomly. I could have turned to the left and gone three miles out of my way and never have seen any of the people that I met. I had acknowledged Jesus, and He had directed my steps. As a result, lives were changed and the kingdom of God went forth.

Embracing Absurdity

In my mind, one reason that this narrative is compelling that it is being recorded by a man who was a committed, existential atheist. One of the benefits of my growing up in the 60's and graduating from high school in 1962, is that I was introduced to the need for revolution. The culture of our parents was condemned by our age group. We decided that the ticky-tacky houses and the self-focused pursuit of careers were not for us. We wanted more. We wanted to get on the "high" way. We traveled. We did drugs. We pursued pleasure to the nth degree. Ultimately this led to the Jesus People revival where hippies with long hair were redeemed by the universal revolutionary Man who turned the world upside down, Jesus.

At 63 years of age, I have lived in two totally separate universes. Now that doesn't mean that I had a home outside of the galaxy. I am talking about universes that are defined by how we look at the world,

He Inclined His Ear

by our world view. For 28 years my world view was dictated by what I could see with my eyes and perceive with my natural mind.

I was born in the middle of World War II. My father was in a foxhole in Germany. My earliest memories of his return from World War II include the nation-wide fear associated with the Cold War and the knowledge that some of my neighbors' loved ones had died in a foreign land. At a very early age, I was conscious of the fact that something dreadful had occurred in the lives of people in my community.

Because our household was not churched or pursuing kingdom principles and purposes, I was very comfortable with godlessness. I was 23 years old before I ever met an adult male who did not use alcohol to be social. Migrating from beer to drugs was a very natural progression for me.

God, religion, and the Bible were not central features in our household. I can honestly say there were only three times in the first 28 years of my life where I offered what I considered to be real prayers. That is not to say that I did not participate in congregational prayers. I did that. I read aloud from prayer books during church services. I even offered extemporaneous prayers at various youth meetings, but this was all done within the expectations of religious tradition.

The three prayers that I offered from my heart are as follows:

When I was eight years old, I was told that my great-grandfather was very sick. I remember him and his garden half a mile outside of our village. He would sit with his neighbor in the shade of several large trees on the edge of the garden plot. He would chew tobacco, spit the juices into a tin can near his chair and watch the corn grow. He had a cane and was obviously very old. He loved me. He took me with him often, and I would sit on his knee. When I heard that he was dying, I cried out, "God, don't let my Gramps die." In 24 hours he was dead. This had a marked influence on my attitude toward prayer. I had no concept that the Lord requires us to pray "in His will." Obviously it was not His will for my great-grandfather to live.

Eight years later at age 16, I was weeks away from totally rejecting Christianity and divorcing myself from the things of the church. I was

W. Stephen Keel

in a boat on a lake in the Adirondack Mountains. My parents had rented a cabin. My mother and two sisters were there. My father was installing cabinets in a school close by. He came to the cabin in the evenings. Normally I would have been fishing with him, but he wasn't there. I took the boat out and fished diligently. I had been on the lake for 3 days and hadn't had a single strike. In an idle moment of dissatisfaction, I said, "God, if You are really God, You could cause me to catch a fish at any time You wanted to. As a matter of fact, You could cause me to catch a fish right now. So let me see You make me catch a fish!"

Instantly I had a strike and I reeled in a fish! In all, I fished five days in a row, and that was the only fish that I caught. You might have thought that that event would have an influence on my attitude toward prayer, but I have to admit, I was like the nine lepers that were healed. I was not like the one that turned around and gave glory to God.

I dismissed the results of that prayer, but I never forgot it. It wasn't until I was 28 years old when I finally bowed to Jesus. The third prayer was a prayer of confession and repentance. It was a sincere cry that the Lord would forgive me and allow me to serve Him. Although I was not living in relationship with Him or calling on His name or seeking His face, clearly He was never un-interested in me. If He had been un-interested in me, I would not be telling these stories.

I had received a degree in English literature with a minor in philosophy and religion. I found an upper level course in existentialism to be life directing. I longed to identity with Descartes and simply say, "I think, and therefore I am."

This desire grew out the feeling of being disenfranchised by the church I had known growing up as a boy. My father had seen the horrors of World War II up close. His first days in Europe were spent building coffins for 1000's of men who had died on D-Day. He spent time in the Battle of the Bulge in the middle of the winter seeking comfort and warmth from a fellow soldier as they were blanketed together underneath the snow. He arrived in Germany in time to experience the final days of the Jewish death camps. A friend of his was shot between the eyes as he and another friend walked along a road in post-war Germany. He was never proud of his part of what

He Inclined His Ear

happened to the sniper that had killed his friend. He and others of his age were not very interested in the things of God. His basic conclusions were that of the age. If God existed, He wouldn't permit the kind of absurdity and chaos that they had seen in war.

In 1966, Daniel Berrigan, a Jesuit Priest, declared authoritatively via national media that "God is dead." I was not able to agree with him. For God to be dead, He would have had to be alive at some time or other, and I was not willing to accept that He ever was.

In spite of feeling disenfranchised, when my dad returned from the war, he chose to make a commitment to the church. I think he did it in part because his kids were growing up. When I was 12, we began attending church, and my father submitted himself to baptism in the Presbyterian Church.

For the next two years dad participated in the affairs of the church, only to become disillusioned again by the lack of integrity that he found on the board of deacons. His negative experiences contributed to my own evaluation of the value of Christianity. For many years my dad declared that Christians were the most dishonest people he had dealt with in the world of business.

When I was 15, I became aware of an adulterous relationship between a member of the church's elder board and a female member of the choir. It appeared that everyone knew about it, but no one seemed to think that this might be sin.

I heard the preacher say clearly that the Bible was purely metaphorical in value. There was no point in attributing truth to the book of Genesis. He said we were all educated enough to know that Genesis was not a reasonable story. He said that there was value, if we listened with a poetic ear. By doing this, we could be encouraged and strengthened through our exposure to the Bible. Naturally, we should believe this preacher since he had traveled to Scotland to study in the best Presbyterian seminaries.

This type of reasoning helped me to justify my self-imposed excommunication from Christianity. At age 16, I was attending church camp as a Vice Moderator of the West District of the Cayuga Syracuse Presbytery. With a title like that, you would have thought I was a really good Christian, but on a particular Thursday night, I looked up at the sky. I saw the vastness of the universe and I concluded that it wasn't possible for God to have manifested Himself as a Man. He would not have recorded it in a book or have anything to do with the framework of human relationships in the organization called the "church."

I made a clear decision to divorce myself from all traditions of religion and to seek knowledge and truth outside of what I had judged to be false. This decision contributed to my giving up the pursuit of a career in engineering and led me to study literature and philosophy.

I concluded that the literary mind was more apt to be seeking truth than the mind of an engineer, so I pursued literature. I soon discovered that Ernest Hemingway, despite his success and popularity, found his solace in a shotgun stuffed in his mouth. William Faulkner, facing remarkable success, drank himself to death. Sherwood Anderson, the proclaimed writer of short stories, died randomly by choking on a toothpick. A leading literary critic of the day, Gertrude Stein, felt it appropriate to label this depressed generation as the generation of the "living dead!" I did not know at the time that the Apostle Peter had written to the church telling them that they were dead in trespasses and sin.

In fact, my attitude was being molded by a number of different forces. In the 1950's, I can remember certain mornings after my parents purchased our first television set.... this was quite a remarkable event because prior to TV, we had listened to the radio for family entertainment. The TV was captivating.

One of the first items of real interest on TV was the launching of rockets in an effort to respond to the Russians who had put "Sputnik," their satellite, into orbit around the earth. The space race was on. There was quite a joke among us because whenever the USA endeavored to launch a satellite, the rocket went up only so far and then, on national TV, where everyone could see it, it fell over on its side and crashed into the ocean. The by-word was "Well, here we go again; back to the drawing board!"

"Back to the drawing board" and the space race produced an amazing educational push. The leaders of the country knew that our capabilities in the space race were tied to our educational system. On every front, efforts were made to examine how we taught various subjects. Mathematics was primarily taught by rote, but the "space challenge" convinced many that we needed to teach the reasoning behind mathematics. New Math came into the classroom with a flourish. Similarly, chemistry was being taught by memorizing the Periodic Tables and formulas, but now we needed to really understand the dynamics of the chemicals, so chemistry was taught more metaphorically.

My 1962 graduating class had been a test bed for many of these new subjects. Even while we were being given this invigorating approach to education, we were being thoroughly indoctrinated in the world of evolution. Our biology class was not the only place where I was taught evolution.

No teacher in the school system considered evolution to be a theory, in spite of the fact that it was known as the "theory of evolution". It was taught as fact and we believed it. By the time I graduated from high school, I was a committed rationalist. I had determined that there was no such thing as spiritual reality. I saw everything in the light of cause and effect.

I had learned from Carl Marx that religion was the opiate of the people. It was easy for me to understand the concept that mortal man, facing complexity and chaos, would need to protect himself or insulate himself against the vastness of the unknown by creating religion. I easily accepted the idea that religion was simply the effort of man to mollify his fears, to protect himself from the complexity and enormity of the universe.

My studies in existentialism introduced me to Albert Camus and his novel "The Stranger." In "The Stranger," the protagonist relates his experiences from a prison cell. He causes to pass before his mind the memory of himself on a beach with a gun in his hand. There was an individual standing in front of the gun. Without remorse or conscience and without even having a clear reason for doing so, he pulled the trigger, killing a man. Having reviewed the activity in his mind from sitting in the prison cell, he asked himself, if he had the opportunity to do it again, would he do anything differently? The conclusion was that he would not! There was no reason for doing anything differently.

He had performed (I learned in a philosophy class) what profound existentialists referred to as a "phenomenological reduction." He had chosen to cleanse his mind and emotions of all tradition, rules, mores, folkways, philosophy and religion, and began with a clean slate, a tabularaza, a mind that wasn't constrained by previous patterns of thought. From this standpoint of emptiness, he found that he had no restraints. There was nothing in his conscience to restrain himself from any activity that would be considered by others to be cruel or immoral or illegal.

Reading that passage had a profound effect on me. Although I did not jump into a life of murder via guns, neither did I fear the law nor man nor human convention nor restraint. I was happy to kill others with my tongue. One time, I told a girl that the reason I had not dated her was that she was "too fat." She responded by telling the people at the party we were attending that I was a narcotics agent. That explained why everyone left the party in a hurry. My tongue placed me in danger and I thought it was funny.

I chose to live a life as my own god. I created my own ontology. Like many men, I concluded that God does NOT reward men either for good or evil. The best way to describe my conclusions about life was that we live in utter absurd chaos, and we do it willingly. Consequences for our actions are purely random or created according to the needs of men to form some sort of order for society.

Chapter 2: Wives First

Several events occurred before I received the Lord, events that began to wake me up to the possibility that there was a spiritual dimension, that God really did exist and that He interacted with men in a very personal way.

On a winter evening, my wife and I were in our home in Amherst, Virginia, living with my mother-in-law. We had returned recently from Alaska where we had taught school and lived as gypsies literally sleeping under the wing our Cessna 180 airplane in the summers.

I was proud of my financial responsibility. We had succeeded in saving money and buying an airplane with cash. We were debt free and had the means to go where we wanted to go and do what we wanted to do. On this night, I was looking over my cash and adding up a few small bills. I discovered that I owed $89 and it was owed now. At that moment, I did not have $89. Nancy's pursuit of the things of the spirit had resulted in her contact with a Presbyterian minister. Roger Bush often spoke about hearing the voice of God. I had very little contact with this man, but my wife had attended his church on Sundays. He was aware of me and knew something of our family

On our $89 night, Roger came to our house with his wife and 4 small children. They were bundled up against the cold. I remember their enthusiasm as they entered the house. He said, "I am not here long. I am glad to meet you, Steve. I wanted to let you know that Sunday at church, there was a lady who gave me a letter with some money in it, and she asked me to use it for the glory of God. I prayed about it and the Lord said to give this to Steve and Nancy Keel. So, here I am, in obedience to God, and here is the envelope. This is for you, and God bless you. Good night." And they left.

We opened up the envelope, and inside was exactly $89 in cash. I was provoked by this, not convinced, but provoked by this. There was an obvious connection between the $89 dollars we needed and the $89 that had been supplied.

Years later I heard the rest of the story. Pastor Roger was really looking forward to receiving his pay check at the end of the month. He had run out of cash and had various needs for his family. At the top of the list was the need to have his washing machine repaired. His wife had a baby in diapers. This was before the days of disposable diapers and not being able to wash diapers was a mini-crisis. He told me that he had received the $89, and God had spoken to him to give it all to us. His wife had spoken to him and reminded him that she needed the washing machine repaired.

Roger asked the Lord if he could take half of the $89 and use it to fix the washing machine and give the other half to Steve and Nancy. The machine had broken down a few months previously, and he knew that the part needed to fix it cost $35. Despite Roger's plea, the Lord said no, give it all to Steve and Nancy.

After he had been obedient in giving us the money, he called the hardware store, hoping that they would allow him to buy the part and pay for it at the end of the month. He described the problem and asked about the part. They asked the age of the washing machine. He said it was less than a year old. They asked how he knew the price of the part. He said that he had had that problem before. They had repaired it for $35, and now it needed the same repair again.

They said to him, "Well, you shouldn't have bought the first part. This machine was under warranty, and you won't have to pay for that part today. We will give you another part, and we will give you your money back for the first repair."

The Lord honored Roger's obedience to the voice of God by doing what he was told to do. I learned the outcome of this story after I became a Christian.

It has taken me some time to get around to telling the story about how I received the Lord. I guess there are several reasons for that. One is that it is not a short story and there's a lot of detail. There's always a question in my mind which detail is important and which detail is just myself rattling on, but I am going to try to tell the story.

It began as I have already stated with two prayers, one unanswered and one answered. The unanswered prayer was the one in which I asked the Lord to heal my great-grandfather. He died. As many as eight years later I prayed a second time complaining. I had been fishing for three days and hadn't even gotten a bite. If He was really God, He could cause me to catch a fish, and at that moment, I caught a fish. I was impressed, but not enough to change my attitude toward God, the Bible and the church.

I was so convinced that there was no spiritual reality, and not only did I deny Christianity, I denied spiritism, witchcraft, Eastern religion, and anything having to do with the spiritual realm. This denial had to be stubbornly maintained, especially around my wife. Nancy had played with a Ouija board as a child. Also, she would tell how she and her cousin, Lillian, had placed their hands on the surface of a small table and "walked" it about the room. Such unbiblical activities were normal in her community, in spite of its outward show of Christianity.

Nancy was very comfortable with the idea that there was a spiritual reality. She too had rejected Christianity because of the hypocrisy she had seen in the church, but she had an intense desire to understand spiritual reality. She was seeking, in her words, the Source of the power or the Ruler of eternity that we meet after death.

In an effort to find the power, she began seeking knowledge of God. In the course of this seeking, she had a vision in the night. In that vision, her father who had committed suicide, appeared to her and told her that she would be with him soon. In another dream she was told that the only thing that could prevent her from being with her father would be if she would seek the name of God. Her experience was very real to her. In a vision, an angel touched her and promised to completely heal her body if she would follow Him all of her life and find His name.

We moved to Alaska and taught elementary classes in very remote villages. One year we taught on the Shumagin Islands on the southern side of the Alaskan peninsula. I spent summers salmon fishing and flying my airplane, and Nancy spent her time seeking the name of God.

For two years, she had sent off to the state library and asked them to forward to her all of the great bibles of the world, the Koran, the Bagavad-Gita, the Upanishads, Book of Mormon, etc. It was her opinion that since these books had been around for some time, she might use them to identify the name of God. She didn't find anyone in those books that struck her as being the true God, but to be academically fair, she decided to turn to the one book that she did not really care to read. The search had to be honest and opened, not biased.

She picked up the Old Testament. As she was reading it, she made a clear observation. She discovered that the Old Testament, unlike the other bibles of the world contained stories about a God who had a personal relationship with the people who were seeking His face and calling on Him to help them. All of the other bibles had been filled with precepts, imaginary stories, illogical sayings and rules. In the Old Testament she discovered that the prophets and King David talked to God and God talked to them. In her heart, she knew that the voice she had heard in her dreams was the same voice as that of God speaking in the Psalms. He had the same character. No other god in the world was like Him.

He was the God of the universe. She wanted a personal relationship with the Creator, so for a period of time she considered herself to be a Jew. The Jewish people prayed to God and read the Old Testament, and she wanted to do that too. She was motivated because her only hope to live a long life was to discover the name of God. This is how she began talking to God.

In Alaska we had a number of "spiritual" experiences in meetings held by a man named Noel Street. He was both a hypnotist and an Eastern philosophy guru. Nancy had read most of the books written by Edgar Cayce, a man who claimed a Christian heritage but also claimed to have a prophetic insight into the future of the world. His books contained prophecies about Atlantis rising again. He focused on apocalyptic events like earthquakes and floods that would affect the coastlines of the world. She eagerly sought to understand the safe and unsafe areas on the earth. Alaska was not safe. According to Edgar Cayce, it would be destroyed around 1990.

When we discovered that we were going to have our first child, we were glad to leave and move back to Virginia. The climate was good and family was close by. I had had bad experiences called flashbacks following an LSD trip. I felt a need to be close to a mental institution.

He Inclined His Ear

Where we were in Alaska, it was 600 miles to the closest strait jacket and that seemed impractical to me.

Nancy knew she had to continue to follow God, and she looked for any person or group that was honestly seeking God. She ruled out Sunday-churchy things, but the only people who seemed to hear from God or to talk to God or to experience the power of God were a small group of ladies who were attending a Presbyterian church pastored by Roger Bush.

Please keep in mind that while she was developing a relationship with these ladies, I was firm in my commitment to rationalism and atheistic existentialism. I worked for a period of time as a corporate pilot. On my last day on the job, I failed to put the landing gear down and made a belly-up landing.

Not being one to be without work, I decided I would be interested in shoeing horses for a living. I flew off to Tennessee in my little airplane and took a crash course in horse shoeing. I returned two weeks later as a farrier.

Nancy was seeking God, and I was seeking everything else. I would ride my horse into remote fields to plant and cultivate marijuana. People I knew were being arrested and going to jail for drugs, and it struck me that that was not a good thing. So, I grew my own and stayed away from people who could get me into trouble. The horseshoeing job enabled me to earn as much as a $100 in a day, which was a considerable sum in those days. Because I was not in debt, I was quite happy with the way things were. I had discovered the fine art of self-medication. I used the precise amounts of pot and beer to be glowing and happy without being overtly drunk or high.

Nancy was relentless searching for the name of God. She began attending Full Gospel Businessmen's Fellowship meetings. The attendees called themselves "Full Gospel" because they considered the gift of speaking in tongues, the manifestation of prophecy and miraculous healings to be evidence of the fullness of the Gospel. They felt that a Gospel that offered just initial salvation was incomplete. They believed that a man could hear from God and encounter the supernatural experiences found throughout the Bible.

There were monthly meetings where businessmen would share testimonies of how God spoke to them, how He healed them or how He healed other people through them. This struck Nancy as being powerful, and she wanted to go where the power was, so she began attending many of these meetings. After several months of nagging, I relented and said I would go with her once. About 150 people attended the meeting. They sang joyously, clapping their hands and enthusiastically expressing their love to Jesus. I sat in the back of the room with a critical eye, unimpressed.

I was unwilling to participate in anything of the sort, but pseudo-casually I observed everything that was going on. At the end of the meeting, the speaker, a Judge Tucker from South Carolina, asked the people about their relationship with Jesus. He said, "If you know Jesus as your Lord and Savior, raise your hand."

Most of the people raised their hands. Then he said, "If you really know Jesus as your Lord and Savior, I want you to stand up right where you are."

Everyone in the room stood up except me. Then he turned to me and said, "Son, I knew you the moment you walked in the door. You are a sinner far from the grace of God, and we are all going to pray for you that you might receive Jesus Christ as your Lord and Savior."

All of a sudden the room broke into pandemonium. Everybody began speaking in tongues, and people gathered around me, laying hands on my shoulders and raising them in the air. They began praying earnestly and fervently for me. In my opinion, it was a ridiculous spectacle. All I could think was, "I have got to get out of here, and I am never coming back to a place like this as long as I live."

I succeeded in getting out and continued to live in self-determination for a season. My wife had told me on several occasions how important it was to her that she discover the name of God. I have already stated the fact that I was a rationalist, an atheistic existentialist. Nonetheless, I began to think that it might be useful for us to find out who this "God" was, but I didn't want to do it just now.

Nancy had two intense experiences. In one of them, she woke in the middle of the night to yet another vision. An apparition of Satan ap-

He Inclined His Ear

peared to her. She saw a dark force come into the room and she knew she was surrounded by the embodiment of pure evil. Her first impression was that he had come to grasp our baby, Rose of Sharon, from the crib in the room. She discovered that he wasn't after the child; he was after her.

The evil force attached itself to her body in such a way that she was in a catatonic state. She was paralyzed. She could not move any part of her body. She could not call for help. She could not even see or hear. She was totally under the power of the evil force and had been reduced to an existence inside of her mind.

The force said to her, "I have your body. Now give me your mind."

She said, "I won't do it."

He said, "I'll wait."

As she waited, the terror of his being was beyond description. The spirit was as a viper with opened mouth and forked tongue flicking several inches from her face, waiting for her to say "yes" so it could lunge into her and kill her. She thought to herself, "What can I do?"

At that moment, it occurred to her that she needed God to save her. Whoever He is, He will have the power to save her. She said inside her mind, "God, come save me!" and waited for Him to respond.

He did. He said, "What is My name?"

She said, "Oh, I have lots of names. I will try them to see which one has the power to save me."

She purposefully started with the ones from the bibles of other religions because she didn't want the God of Christians to be the One. She viewed Christians as people lacking the burning desire for God that she had. She considered them to be without an ounce of power in their lives to do anything.

So she said, "Allah, come save me."

She waited. She spoke the name of Allah again and waited. Nothing happened; Allah didn't come. All the time, she remained encased in evil with the hideous serpent in her face ready to leap into her mind.

Then she said, "Mohammed, come save me."

W. Stephen Keel

Nothing happened. She waited and called his name a second time.

She said, "Krishna, come save me," and repeated the process.

Nothing happened.

She said, "Buddha, come same me." She repeated the process again.

Nothing happened.

She said, "Ra, come save me." Her list of gods was getting shorter!

Nothing happened.

She said, "Maroni, come, save me." What else could she do? Maroni did not come.

After several more names, she could not think of any more, but One. Finally she said, "Jesus, come save me!"

He came in a flash of light, and the demon burst like water and shattered into a million splinters. Nancy came out of her catatonic state and was bathed by the anointing of the Holy Spirit and the presence of God from the top of her head to the tip of her toes. In one fell stroke, she learned that the name of God is Jesus. She now knew the source of all power in this world and the next. She also learned the names of everyone one who was NOT God! Scripture says the stone the builders rejected has become the chief cornerstone....how true!

I was sleeping beside her, and she woke me up to tell me what had happened. I have to admit that I thought it was an interesting story, but I told her to go back to sleep...enough of this foolishness! That story triggered a switch inside of me. I began to realize that her seeking of the name of God and now her identification with this person Jesus Christ was having a definite bad effect on my life style.

Chapter 3: From the World of Darkness into the Light

It was not reasonable for me to live a carefree, sinful life around this Jesus stuff. I considered my alternatives. I made a decision. I decided to leave my wife and child and let them follow Jesus. I'd go my own way. I pondered the decision through the night. The next morning I waited for the right moment to tell her. I took her outside on the porch and sat her down.

I said, "Look, I have something I have got to discuss with you. Our lives have drifted apart, more than I can manage. You are in love now with this Jesus guy, and I thought you were supposed to be in love with me. This Jesus guy is not compatible with my lifestyle. I have concluded that the best way to handle this situation is to leave. My bag is packed. You are here with your mother. You'll be taken care of, and I am going to live the life that was designed for me to live."

As I delivered this message to her and prepared to leave, Roger Bush pulled into the driveway. We lived in the country about three and a half miles from Amherst. As best I recall, this was the second time he had been to our house. The first time was when he delivered the $89 I told you about previously.

Roger Bush got out of the car and shook his head as he walked across the yard toward the porch. He was muttering to himself as he approached. He said, "I just don't understand it. I have been trying to get to Elon, Virginia, for two weeks, and I know the Lord has told me to go to Elon, but when I got to the traffic circle in Amherst, the Lord spoke to me and said, 'Go, see Steve and Nancy.' I don't understand what's happening. I know I am supposed to go to Elon. I drove around the circle three times telling the Lord where I was supposed to go, but He kept saying, 'Go, see Steve and Nancy.'"

This muttering from the man who brought me the $89 definitely interested me. I was curious as to what this was all about, but I also had an attack mode that I used often when talking to Christians. I began attacking him saying, "I don't where you are getting off with all this stuff about hearing God talking to you, but here is something that I know. You Christian people are basically weak-minded. You are afraid to face the chaos of the universe, so you have invented this Jesus myth as a form of solace, some kind of anchor for your soul. I want you to know I don't need an anchor. I am like a ship at sea and my sails are filled with the wind. I am not afraid of the unknown directions I might go. And, that's exactly what I am about right now; I am allowing that wind to blow in my life. I appreciate the fact that you have come out here, and it is a very interesting story that you are telling, but I don't want anything to do with it."

Roger Bush left, but I didn't.

My wife admitted afterwards that while all of this had been going on, starting when I began telling her I was going to leave, she had begun to pray. She had hoped upon hope that something would happen to prevent me from leaving. She was rejoicing in the fact that Roger was there. She had wanted desperately to call Roger Bush, but she knew that I would leave immediately if she touched the phone, so she prayed for a miracle to reach Roger before I left. When he pulled into the driveway, her heart was filled with relief that somehow the situation would come to a good end. Here is a time when God answered a prayer by speaking to another person and telling them to do something. God made the problem too big for Nancy to handle so that He might display Himself in greater measure using someone else's help.

I now found myself with an increased need to discover the reality of God, so I made an agreement with my wife, "Let's settle this matter once and for all. I have doggedly resisted all of your efforts to delve into spiritual reality. If there is a spiritual reality, I want to know about it. If there is a God, I want to know about that also."

One of the practices that we had learned in our seeking had to do with dietary reform. For one particular period of two years, we ate what was called a Macrobiotic Diet which consisted primarily of brown rice and vegetables. We were trying to get the Yin and the Yang of our bodies aligned by what we were eating.

I also had been introduced to the health benefits of fasting. I had fasted one time for a week as a non-Christian, strictly for health purposes.

He Inclined His Ear

So I said to my wife, "Let's get away from here. I think there is too much clutter in the air around here with all these weird Christians. Let's drive to Florida and let's enter into a period of fasting and seeking the name of God and the face of God, and if He really exists, He will show Himself to us and we can settle this matter."

She agreed to go.

It is interesting that though she already knew the name of God, her testimony didn't convince me one iota. I had to find it out for myself. We packed up our goods and our small child, Rose of Sharon, and drove our station wagon to Florida. (Rose of Sharon had been named after a character in John Steinbeck's novel, "Grapes of Wrath." We later discovered that it came originally from the "Song of Solomon".)

As it happened, Noel Street, the guru with whom we had attended meetings in Alaska, lived in Florida. Since he was purportedly a spiritual man, it seemed reasonable to me to visit him and ask his advice regarding my quest. We went to his office and he told us what we were doing was a reasonable thing to do.

He said, "I'd like to help you. In fact I have a mobile home close to the beach about 30 miles from here. I'd be glad to give you the keys to this mobile home, and you can stay there and pursue your search for God. And, by the way, don't become too interested in that Christianity stuff. Although the Bible is a good book and has a lot of good information, the people who use it are messed up and don't have much spiritual depth or insight."

With those instructions, we went to his place. Shortly after we arrived, he arrived also. He said, "I thought I'd just be here while you are here. I don't want to interrupt. I am going fishing most of the time. Say, Steve, how would you like to go fishing with me?"

He took me to the beach and we fished together. I was fasting and everything was going along quite well. I felt good about seeking knowledge of God.

On the third day, he went fishing again, but he went by himself this time. While he was gone, I began plundering his library and other materials. He had a collection of 33rpm records. One in particular interested me. It was on the subject of Theosophy. As I listened to this record, the speaker discussed the philosophy of Theosophy. He spoke of a Cosmic Christ, the one that embraced all the religions of the world and of a religion that was inclusive toward all people. This cosmic Christ wasn't given over to creating conflict and dissension among spiritual people. The teachings of Theosophy were based on esoteric knowledge in the possession of an ancient people. This knowledge could bring one into a far greater relationship with the universe than any other way.

As I listened to this, I thought, "Well, that is the answer to my prayers."

The cultural Jesus, that dominates the world of Christianity that I had been exposed to, was clearly of little value. Noel Street had said that, but now, I too understood. We have a "Cosmic Christ" and he has been discovered by those seeking for esoteric knowledge throughout the millennia. The Rosicrucian sects and other mystics had found this knowledge, too. They had found the "truth", and now I had found the "truth", also. I said to Nancy, "This is it. This is what I am looking for. I'm a Theosophist, and I know the Cosmic Christ."

I was so impressed by the long-playing record and the information on it, I said, "Look, what we need to do is make a copy of this message onto a cassette so we can take it home with us. Surely there is some way we can do it."

We plundered the trailer, and I was able to find patch cords, a cassette recorder and some empty cassettes. I was able to record the message. I broke my fast because I had what I was looking for, and I said, "Let's go home."

I wasn't a very polite individual; it never occurred to me, that we should leave a thank you note or in any way acknowledge Noel Street's hospitality. We packed up and drove out the driveway taking a turn toward the beach because the highway we needed to take north was near the beach. Just after we turned, we met Noel Street driving toward us. He waved. We stopped and got out of the car. I listened as my wife began to interrogate him. She said, "Do you ever do astral traveling, going about the world teaching your students?"

He Inclined His Ear

He said, "Yes, I do. I allow my body to be used for that sometimes. That is characteristic of the way I work with my students." Then he turned to me, and he said, "Stephen, did you get what you came here for? Did you enjoy transferring the Theosophy information from the record to the cassette?"

When he said that, I was dumfounded. I knew that he had not been anywhere near the trailer while I was recording the message from the record. I knew the exact spot on the beach where he was fishing, so I knew where he had been. I was amazed at his spiritual insight, knowledge and power. He had seen into my circumstances supernaturally. I was quite impressed! I developed a new eagerness to know more about this kind of power.

We returned to Virginia. I was like a typical convert. I was really enthusiastic about seeking any form of spiritual manifestation that might be remarkable. I met with an elderly black man who dabbled in what was called "roots." He could read roots and tell fortunes. He was able to heal people using these "fortune roots" and various incantations.

I was so convinced of his power that I invited him to travel with us to the hospital in Charlottesville, where my wife's aunt was lying in bed with a debilitating form of rheumatoid arthritis. I brought him into the room in the context of Southern culture where the whites and blacks have a well-defined relationship with each other. That didn't necessarily include ministry; a white woman receiving ministry from a black man, but my wife's aunt was so desperate, she was willing to endure whatever was necessary. He said his incantations and prayed, but as it happened, nothing came from it. I was disappointed with my first real experiment with spiritual power.

Shortly after this my wife had another vision in the night. In this vision, Noel Street appeared to her and said, "There is going to be an earthquake in your area within three days. Everything is going to be destroyed. The epicenter of the quake is underneath your home and you must leave immediately. Anything you take with you will be saved, but anything you leave behind will be totally destroyed."

Nancy woke up at 5am, <u>terrified</u> by the vision. When she told me the vision, I remembered Noel Street knowing I was copying his Theosophy record, but I was still skeptical, especially since my "roots" man had not performed well.

I said, "Oh, man, this is really weird!"

My wife, feeling a tremendous urgency, called Roger Bush on the phone right away and shared the vision with him. He said, "We understand that this man who came to you in the vision is not a Christian. In fact, he is an anti-Christ. It's not necessary for us to fear him or to even listen to what he has to say. The Biblical pattern is for a Christian to remain and to stand firm and to hold his place. Evil must move away, not the other way around."

But then he said, "Wait, God is speaking to me. I have a word from the Lord for both you and Steve. The Lord has said, 'My hand is upon you. I have a work I must do and you must go.' Amen. In this case, you need to leave."

She told me what he said. I am thinking, "We've got to do something." Now I was beginning to wonder if something might happen.

I agreed to pack up our belongings and to leave. Nancy woke her mother up and told her the story. Her mother shared her fear. We loaded her family heirlooms….dishes, mirrors, pictures….as much as we could fit into the back of a big old truck I owned. Along with all of our earthly belongings of value, we decided to take her mother about 10 miles away to her aunt's place. I was still skeptical.

I told Nancy, "I have a horse to shoe in Gretna. Go ahead and drive the truck away from here. I suggest you go up to Charlottesville, to Oak Leigh. At one of your Full Gospel meetings, there was a man who seemed to be moderately intelligent, and he claimed to have knowledge of spiritual things. I think we need to go to that retreat center that he was talking about and present your vision and the prophecy. Let's see if he thinks there is any value or meaning to it."

She agreed.

Nancy drove the truck to Charlottesville about 55 miles away. I got in the car and headed off to shoe horses. My appointment was for early afternoon, and I stopped at a friend's house on the way just because he had horses and he was a friend. This visit was typical of my

He Inclined His Ear

life style. As I arrived at Dick Putt's house, I discovered that there was a Baptist preacher trying to share the Gospel with him. When I arrived, I was "red meat". He was all over me for spiritual conquest. He asked, "Do you mind if I ride with you to Gretna while you shoe the horse?"

Like a lamb to the slaughter, I said, "No, I don't mind. I could use the company."

For the next four hours, he preached the Gospel of Jesus Christ to me. I am sure that he told me everything he knew. He read many Scriptures to me. Every step along the way, I defied him and I denied him. I was never so happy in my life to get rid of this guy. I was convinced he was totally full of baloney. I wanted nothing to do with anything with which he was associated. I continued on to Oak Leigh, the retreat center where Nancy had driven.

The man we were hoping to speak to, Bob Manzano, was not available. He was on a trip and would be returning the next day. We were invited to spend the night. Oak Leigh was a Christian retreat center and there were plenty of facilities for our small family.

The following day was Sunday. There was a worship service with about 300 people present. The service lasted three hours and manifested an exuberance that was remarkable. I detected an angelic beauty. At one point in the service, I heard a voice beside me. It was a woman singing and it was extraordinarily beautiful. My eyes were shut at the time, and I pictured in my mind what she might look like....some young lovely girl. When I opened my eyes and looked, I saw she was one of those ticky-tacky, middle-age American women that our generation of hippies had ridiculed. Her hair was done up in a repulsive Barbie Doll manner. Her clothes were strictly polyester. There was nothing about her that was of any interest to me, except the song I had heard. I made a mental note to try at a later time to explain the contradiction between her beautiful singing and her ugly appearance.

The worship service ended and the people had a community meal together. There were quite a few hippies in the crowd...people with long hair and sandals. I was comfortable with being around the hippies. So in spite of the polyester woman, I didn't feel too bad about being there. We were given an appointment to meet with Bob Manzano at seven o'clock that evening. We spent the afternoon on the grounds of the mansion where everyone was enjoying themselves in fellowship.

At seven o'clock that evening we went upstairs to his apartment on the second floor over the sanctuary. Oak Leigh at one time had been owned by the Maxwell House family, the coffee people. The building was an old Southern mansion that had been purchased by a non-profit group to hold Christian meetings and to provide a retreat center with accommodations for young people who were seeking God.

Our interview began. We shared both the prophecy and the dream. When we finished speaking, Bob said, "The Bible is very clear. If a prophecy is of the Lord, it will come to pass. If it doesn't come to pass, you don't need to fear the prophet. Since this prophecy has a three-day time limit, and yesterday and today are already past, I suggest that stay here through tomorrow. Contact your people in Amherst. Check things out and go back home."

That seemed like a very reasonable thing to do, so I agreed to do that.

Then he turned to me and said, "Is there any reason why Jesus Christ should not be the Lord of your life?"

That was a VERY provocative question. For 28 years, particularly the last 12, I had thousands of reasons why Jesus Christ should not be the Lord of my life. At that moment, I couldn't think of a single one, so I answered honestly, "No."

He said, "Pray with me."

I said, "Okay."

He had me repeat a sinner's prayer. He had me say, "I'm a sinner. I repent. I believe that Jesus Christ died on the cross for the forgiveness of my sins. I believe that He was crucified and died and was buried and arose again the third day. When He arose, He made a way for me to go to heaven and to live eternally with Him. Jesus, please forgive me for my sins and be the Lord of my life."

As I muttered these words, I was physically thrown to the floor by the Spirit of God. I was soon down on my knees, gagging, laughing,

He Inclined His Ear

coughing and convulsing. Finally I was able to stand up. Bob looked at me and said, "You are a Christian now."

And I said, "You are full of baloney!"

As a matter of fact, I may have used a different word, but I have been reformed, so I am not using it now.

"You Christians have got it all wrong. You think that Jesus is the only way, the truth and the life, and that no man can come to the Father any other way except through Him."

You see, in my quest, I had started reading the New Testament. I had gone all the way through Matthew, Mark, Luke and John. I read the book of Acts, but I was completely boondoggled when I got to the book of Romans, so I had given up the pursuit of the New Testament at that point. At least I knew what Christians had *thought* the truth was. I said, "I've been a student of religion and philosophy for a number of years, and one thing I am clear on: Jesus is *not* the only way to come to God. There are many religions, and there are many pathways to God!"

Mr. Manzano turned to me, and rather than argue with me, he simply said, "I appreciate your opinion, but according to the Word of God, and according to the prayer you just prayed, you have just received Jesus Christ as your Lord and Savior. You are now a Christian!"

Just as I couldn't think of any reason why Jesus shouldn't be the Lord of my life, I couldn't think of any way to debate what he had just said to me. In a conciliatory way, I said, "If you want me to say that I am a Christian, okay, I'm a Christian. I have grown up in the United States of America, a place that calls itself a Christian nation. I had experiences as a young man attending Christian churches. I took part in everything they offered. If you want me to be a Christian, I can do that. I'll be a Christian."

All along I was looking for a way out of the conversation. He said, "Okay," with no further comment.

He let us go, and we went back to our room for the night.

W. Stephen Keel

Topsy Turvy – My World Flip Flops

The next day I recall standing by the side of the trailer that I pull behind my car that housed the equipment that I used to shoe horses. I was in a state of utter confusion. I could not put two and two together. I could not figure out why I was knocked on the floor when I prayed a sinner's prayer. I could not understand the exclusive nature of Jesus. It seemed to me that He ought to be more inclusive if He wanted to be popular.

In an act of futility, I said, "I give up."

I went inside the building to the kitchen area where several people were eating breakfast. A man was sitting there who had a cross on a chain around his neck. He was a strong young man. I was a strong young man, so I thought I would confront him. I said, "I see you are one of those stupid Christians. You've got that cross around your neck."

He looked at me and said, "You know what your problem is, you don't believe in the book of Genesis."

That's the way he opened the conversation.

I said, "Of course, I don't believe in the book of Genesis. No thinking person in society today has any interest in the myths and fables contained in the book of Genesis."

Peter Zarcone began to reveal to me the teachings of scientific creationism. Today this is referred to as "Intelligent Design." He took me through the relevance of the flood and the earth being covered by canopy of water that opened up causing a deluge. He spoke of rain falling on earth for the first time, and how the climate had been like a greenhouse until the flood occurred. After the flood, the greenhouse effect went away, and new dynamics of air movement brought about conditions where glaciers were formed. The dinosaurs were killed. He covered a litany of biological events that I had previously only heard explained from the perspective of evolutionary thought. Had I not been knocked on the floor, the night before, I am certain that I could not have listened to Peter's lecture. I did not know at the time that Jesus taught, "Unless a man is born again, he cannot see the kingdom of God."

He Inclined His Ear

In the course of his dissertation at a special moment, it was as if I had been standing in a room filled with darkness. Someone had walked in and flipped the wall switch, flooding the room with light. My mind and my spirit were flooded with the realization that Genesis was a valid book. Not only was Genesis true, but John 14 was true also. When Jesus said, "I am the way, the truth and the light, no man can come to the Father except by Me." It was as accurate and as true a statement as those found in the book of Genesis.

When the light went on, I turned to this Peter and I said, "Shut up! I have heard enough. I have got to go outside and do something." That "shut up" remark was characteristic of my lack of graciousness. I went outside and sat underneath a huge oak tree.

I said, "Lord, Jesus, I have been wrong all of these years. I have criticized You, Your Bible, Your people. It was a huge mistake. I was living in a state of deception. I now see that You are the Lord of the universe, and I ask You please, please forgive me. Not only forgive me, but receive me as Your disciple. Allow me to submit to You as the Lord of my life, and I will follow You all the days of my life."

I stood up from that prayer a changed man. I headed back inside the building. At the front door was another young man who had recently been saved. He had played football for the University of Miami. He saw the light in my eyes, and he became excited as he realized what had happened to me. He gave me a huge bear hug and lifted me up off the ground. Suddenly my heart was flooded with love for these people and this place and for Jesus.

Later I learned that the Scripture taught, "By this we know that we have been translated from the world of darkness into the world of light, because we have love for the brethren."

I had discovered love for the brethren. The intensity of my new life in Christ picked up rapidly. That evening, Bob Manzano taught a Bible study where he discussed the value of obedience to the voice of God. This was the very first Bible study I participated in as a brand new Christian. When babies are born they are said to bond with their mothers. I am somewhat eager to discuss the benefits and realities of hearing the voice of God because in my new spiritual life I was instantly and radically bonded to the concept.

W. Stephen Keel

The Bible study was taken from the Old Testament where Joshua was confronted by the commander of the armies of the Lord of Heaven. He was given instruction regarding obedience. When the Bible study was over, Peter Zarcone opened up the Bible to Romans chapter 6. He showed me that a person who is now a Christian can be buried in baptism, reflecting the death of Christ, and raised in the likeness of the resurrection of Christ. I saw the picture immediately, and I said that I wanted to be baptized. Had I known or remembered the jailer and his family in the book of Acts, I would have demanded immediate baptism. I had just heard a teaching on hearing the voice of God and obeying immediately.

I submitted to an agreement that I would be baptized at daybreak the following morning.

I went to bed and fell asleep finding myself in a vision, seeing person after person whom I had known over the last 12 years. I saw many that I had hurt with my insensitive tongue. I saw people I had criticized and offended. I asked them in the vision to please forgive me for my gross attitudes and actions. This went on for hours; situation after situation, person after person. I felt a great sorrow for the sin that was upon me. At a certain point, I became exhausted, and I said, "Lord, I know You are the Author of this experience I am having, but I can't take it anymore. I am exhausted. Please stop this vision and allow me to sleep?"

Almost immediately I fell into a deep sweet sleep. I didn't need an alarm clock to wake me up. I got up at the break of dawn. My wife, Peter and I wandered out to a farm pond a short distance from Oak Leigh. As the sun rose and covered the mountains with light near Charlottesville, Virginia, Peter explained that he was going to baptize me in the name of the Father, the Son and the Holy Spirit, and in the name of Jesus.

The reason for that particular formula was due to certain Christians who used different Scriptures for the names of God in the baptism. He thought that maybe he could overcome any controversy by combining the names of God from two separate references to baptism, so he baptized me in the name of the Father, the Son and the Holy Spirit, and in the name of Jesus. When I came out of the water, I was refreshed and

He Inclined His Ear

renewed. This moment marked the beginning of the rest of my life as a Christian. While the dawn was very quiet and peaceful, my new birth was a radical and violent departure from the old " Steve Keel".

At this point both Roger Bush's and Noel Street's prophecies were being fulfilled, but I didn't know it. I'll explain that later.

The day of my baptism, I had another opportunity to shoe horses nearby. The horse kicked me. It kicked me so hard that I could barely walk. I returned to Oak Leigh for more fellowship, prayer time, and Bible study. At the end of the Bible study, I asked if the people would pray for me, which they did. As I walked up the stairs to our bedroom, I dragged my injured leg one step at a time. I could barely walk. I was engulfed with pain. The next day I woke up, and I was totally and completely healed. I realized that I had been healed in the wonderful and precious name of Jesus Christ, my new-found Savior and Lord.

That day I went out to another horseshoeing job. I stopped by a bar for lunch and had a glass of beer at the luncheon counter, a typical behavior on my part. As I drank the glass of beer, the effect of the alcohol filtered into my body. I realized that it was in conflict with my new felt sensation of the presence of the Holy Spirit. Jesus had come into my body and my endorphins were flowing. These two entities, the alcohol and Jesus, were bumping into each other. They were similar in some ways, but the experience of Jesus was so much more sublime and profound, I made a decision to never drink beer again as long as I live. Close to forty years later, the Lord is still granting me that grace with the exception that I occasionally drink a non-alcoholic beer.

We returned to Amherst. I had been told that the Bible was my "rule book" and I should obey it because it contained the Words of God. On the first Sunday morning after becoming a Christian, I was pondering the question, "Where should I go to church?"

It seemed apparent to me that the commandment to "love my neighbor" meant that I should go to the closest church in the neighborhood. That church happened to be a little black church not far from the place where we were living. It was close enough that I could actually walk to it. I went by myself.

W. Stephen Keel

When I entered, the all-black congregation greeted me. As the only white person in the place, I was a curiosity. They asked me to tell them about myself. On the first Sunday of my Christian life, I stood in the pulpit of a black church and shared the testimony of how I received Jesus Christ as my Lord and Savior. Little did I know that that event was going to be the beginning of a pattern. Years later I would become the only white man preaching on an all-black Gospel radio station in Yanceyville, North Carolina. That preaching would become a world-wide ministry reaching out to people of color in multiple languages and in dozens of nations.

The second Sunday we decided to attend the First Presbyterian Church in Amherst, Virginia, where Roger Bush was the pastor. I had shared the joy of my salvation with Roger since returning from Oak Leigh, and he had invited us to come to church.

I told him, "Look, I have been in a Presbyterian church before, and I know that Presbyterians don't do things in church the same way things are being done at Oak Leigh. They don't worship with the same exuberance and intensity. The fact is that I have had such a profound experience with God; there is no way that I can NOT worship God. I am warning you, when they get to the part where they sing the doxology 'Praise God from whom all blessings flow,' it's not going to be possible for me NOT to praise God. I will have to raise my hands and praise Him with everything that is within me."

He looked at me. I had this long beard and short hair. I was glowing with the light of God. He knew that this was going to unleash something in the church, but he said, "Whatever you have got to do, do it."

We went to the church. After they took up the offering, they began to sing the doxology. Then all six feet two inches and 225 pounds of me stood up, and I raised my hands in the air and worshipped the Lord.

One of the choir members said afterwards that what occurred was so astounding that anything could have happened next; the sky could have opened up, and heaven could have come down in an instant. In other words, there was a violent shaking of the atmosphere in that church that Sunday. By my merely raising my hands and enthusiastically worshipping the Lord, I had challenged the age old spiritual

He Inclined His Ear

atmosphere of restraint. This action became the fulfillment of the prophecy concerning an earthquake in our community.

Clearly Roger had heard correctly, "My children, my hand is upon you. I have a work I must do and you must go."

We had piled into the car and truck and gone to Oak Leigh. Three days later, I was baptized. "Behold, old things were passed away and all things became new."

On the third day, everything we left behind was gone: my alcohol, drugs, cigarettes, profanity, and most importantly, my anger towards Christians.

All of those things were left behind, and that which we took with us remained. That which we took with us was the new-found revelation and understanding of the Person Jesus Christ. We found faith that has remained to this day.

The earthquake was a spiritual shaking that spread out into the vicinity around where I lived. As the months unfolded, I testified many places regarding what the Lord had done for me. What God had destroyed was not the household in Amherst, but the "head of the household". I had been known as a notorious sinner. I had come to this small community and manifested my blatant atheism. Those that knew me knew that I was a wild man! But, that was the old Steve Keel. He died and God raised up a new man who would listen and obey. The new man was seen in church worshipping, declaring the beauty of holiness and the way of salvation!

The following week we went back to church at Oak Leigh. I had read John chapter 14 in its entirety, and I was thoroughly convinced of its value. I asked Bob Manzano if he would mind if I read John chapter 14 to the congregation during the church service. It had come alive to me, and I believed that when I read it, it would be useful for other people to hear. He said, "Yes, that would be fine for you to read it."

Just before he preached his morning message, he asked me to read John, chapter 14. When I finished, he said, "That was a remarkable reading. I know that you understood what you read. Some interesting things have been happening in your life. Why don't you tell the people here what's been happening in your life."

W. Stephen Keel

I shared the story of my agnosticism, atheism and existentialism, and the story about how the Lord had spoken in the night saying "My children, my hand is upon you...."

I told how God had accomplished the work, and I had become a new creature in Christ. When I finished, he turned to the congregation of several hundred people and asked, "Is there anybody here, after having heard this story, who would like to have the same thing come forth in their life?"

Fourteen people responded to the call. They came forward and stood in a circle holding hands. He prayed with them the prayer that I had prayed only three weeks previously; thus, I began a life of hearing the voice of God with an eagerness to obey it. This would mark the first of many Sunday mornings to come, where I would share a convincing message of God's deliverance and love.

Baby Steps in Jesus

There's a special time in a Christian's life when he is a newborn child of God. He has child-like faith. I was blessed with grace to believe God and to expect wonderful things to occur.

One of the first things that happened was I found myself driving about the countryside with an eager, eager desire to serve God. I had a conversation with the Lord; I said, "Lord, I want to do anything that You want me to do; go anywhere that You want me to go; be anything that You want me to be. All I need to begin is for You to speak to me and tell me what to do. I am going to ask You, in the name of Jesus, give me direction right now."

I closed my eyes, listened intently, and I heard a still small voice...mind you, it was a little surprising,...I thought I was on my way to Africa or South America for mission work.....but I heard a still small voice, and it said, "Stop drinking Pepsi Cola."

Instantly I knew it was God. I had lived a life-style of addiction. I had been addicted to alcohol, tobacco, and drugs. I knew that I had been set free from every one of them, but now that I was a Christian, I was pacifying my addictive nature by drinking Pepsi Cola. I was drinking eight or more bottles a day looking for the caffeine buzz. When I

He Inclined His Ear

heard the voice of God telling me to stop drinking Pepsi Cola, I knew it was God. It was _for_ me and not _against_ me. I said "Amen" to God and repented of Pepsi Colas.

Conversations like that occurred on a regular basis.

Shortly after my salvation, Roger Bush found himself in a conflict of belief. The rules of his church did not permit water baptism. This was a practice that was accepted and encouraged among the Full Gospel Businessmen, as well as speaking in tongues. He made the decision very shortly after I received the Lord, to resign from the Presbyterian Church and to form a house church. For months he had been teaching in meetings in Vic Adderton's home in Lynchburg, Virginia. Their home was always filled with people who were hungry for God.

This was in the early 1970's. The Charismatic renewal was in full swing. Mainline church members and Roman Catholic Church members were seeking opportunities to hear the voice of God personally. They were gathering in informal groups around the nation. Nancy and I attended many meetings at Vic Adderton's home.

During one meeting, I experienced something that happened quite frequently during that stage of my Christian life. I found myself subjected to a massive migraine headache. There were spiritual components of my life that were being worked upon. When the Scripture says to work out your own salvation with fear and trembling, that has a lot to do with our being transformed by the renewing of our mind. It has a lot to do with our emotional being, our soul, and our being conformed to the image of Jesus Christ. For that transformation to occur, it requires more than a determination not to drink Pepsi Cola.

I was subject to bad migraine headaches frequently, and this evening, I had a blasting headache. During the worship portion of the gathering, others were ecstatically experiencing the presence of Jesus. I was experiencing this pounding headache. I heard the voice of the Lord directing me to slip across the living room from my seat on the sofa to where a young man, Eric Vess, was sitting in a chair. I knew that I was to get on my knees before him and to ask him to pray for my headache. While the singing was flowing, I obeyed the voice of God.

Eric prayed, asking in the name of Jesus that I be delivered from the headache. I turned to go seven feet back across the room to my seat, and before I sat down, I realized that I was totally and completely delivered from the intense pain of this migraine headache.

In another chapter, we will journey through the world of migraine headaches, but now, I want to tell a story that is very similar to the $89 story.

We were meeting with Christians at various locations in the Amherst and Lynchburg, Virginia areas. Shortly after I was saved a carload of Jesus freaks arrived at our home from Clifton Forge, Virginia. They were talking about seeing angels. They were saying things like "I saw the Lord do this," or "the Holy Spirit did that...."

They had the excitement that was characteristic of what became known as the Jesus movement. Tens of thousands of hippies found God and came into their new life in Christ with thrilling experiences in the Holy Spirit. They were forming Christian communities and developing relationships with each other. They were focused on loving one another so that their joy might be full. And it was.

I was part of all that. The Jesus freaks came to my house, and we worshipped the Lord together. I told them I had a truck being repaired at the local Ford dealership. If they didn't mind, I needed them to give me a ride so that I could pay my bill and pick up the truck. They did not mind.

When we arrived at the Ford place, it occurred to me that in my rapturous attitude toward life, I had neglected to think how much it was going to cost to pay for the repairs. I told them, "I may have a problem. I don't know how much they are going to charge me. Let me see how much money I have."

I opened my wallet and found $71.45. I showed them what I had and asked them to agree with me in prayer that this would be enough money to pay the bill.

We prayed, "Father, in the name of Jesus, please allow this $71.45 to be enough to pay the bill. By the way, I need $2 to put some gas in tank so I can drive it home."

He Inclined His Ear

I went inside the shop, and the cashier pulled out the invoice. As he added it up with tax, I waited expectantly. The total came to $71.45, the exact amount that I had! I gave him the cash and testified to him regarding our prayer. I went back outside and showed the Jesus freaks the invoice amount of $71.45. They had seen me count the money before I went in. In all of the rejoicing, I remembered the gas problem and said. "Wait a minute. Lord, I asked You for $2 to put gas in the tank."

Just as I said that, the young man in the back seat reached in his pocket and pulled out $2 and said here is what you need.

Does God answer prayer? Does God answer prayer directly and specifically? I have experienced event after event where Jesus has answered prayer directly and specifically convincing me that He is not dead, that He is not the god of deism who lives in the fourth universe spying on us through a telescope. He is the God of David who said that His rod and His staff comforts us. God's rod and staff surely comforted me in those early days, and they continue to comfort me today.

To Be a Preacher or Not to Be a Preacher

It is significant that a single conversation can change the course of life of an impressionable young person. In the early summer, when I was 16, the Presbyterian pastor in Upstate New York visited my parent's home. I clearly remember my mother, myself and the pastor seated at the small breakfast table between the kitchen and the garage. My mother had an important question. She asked, "What do the people in the Baptist church mean when they say they have been saved?"

He said, "Well, I am really not sure, but I don't think it is that important. I think it is only something that they talk about to try to distinguish themselves from everybody else."

When I heard him say, "I am really not very sure...," it struck me that that was an unusual response from a man whom I knew had gone to seminary and received an in-depth theological education. That incident coupled with other experiences, birthed in me a profound disrespect for men who were paid to represent God.

W. Stephen Keel

Another thing that prevented me from having an interest in Christianity, was something that I knew about myself. I knew that I wasn't an individual who was satisfied to do something halfway. The logical consequence of becoming a Christian would result in my going to seminary and becoming a pastor. I saw that was the emphasis and direction pursued by virtually anyone I knew that "got religion." I was determined not to follow that pathway.

A week after I received the Lord, I heard an interesting testimony. A man stood in front of a congregation of about 300 people and said, "Last week I was a Baptist preacher. Today I am a sign painter. Let me tell you how wonderful it is to be a sign painter. For years I was frustrated. I loved to tell people about Jesus, but I had a problem. Whenever I began a conversation about the Lord, the first thing they would do is ask me, 'What do you do for a living?' I would reply that I was the pastor of such-and-such church. Inevitably, they would say, 'Oh, now I understand why you are talking to me'. Their eyes would glaze over, and they listened without really listening. Last Friday I resigned my position as pastor, and opened my new business as a sign painter. On Saturday I met a man and began to tell him about Jesus, and he asked me the same question, 'What do you do for a living?' I said, I am a sign painter and he said, 'Oh, tell me more about this Jesus.'"

When I heard that story, I knew it had been prepared for me to hear on that very day. I was now three weeks into my life as a Christian and was already concerned about my need to "preach." That testimony solved the problem as to whether I would have to be a pastor or preacher. I knew then that I could minister the Word of God without joining the ranks of an ecclesiastical group for which I had small respect. Many could easily criticize this position, but I know now and I knew then that the Lord wanted me to walk in the power of the Spirit of God, without setting myself "up" or "aside" in a particular denomination. I knew instinctively that I could demonstrate to others that it is possible to walk in the power of God without becoming a "professional" Christian.

I can't tell you that it has been easy, because it is not easy. Early in my Christian experience, I made a decision to be disciplined in the reading of the Word. One particular Saturday, I saw a gymnast competing in the Olympics. I realized that the only way they could compete at that level of athleticism was through discipline. The same day I saw another individual play a beautiful, but difficult piece on the piano. I knew then that discipline was involved. I made a decisive point to discipline myself in the study of the Word of God. By the enabling grace of God, I have been able to maintain this discipline for almost forty years.

Through my investigation in God's Word, I frequently have received revelation, or some may prefer to call it "illumination". I was gaining insight into the words and ways of God. While it was exciting for me, it was a problem not having anyone with whom to share my insights and excitement. I would go to church meetings. The pastor or the other people who were authorized to do so would speak, and I would sit in frustrated anonymity with the Word of God burning in my heart.

The Lord solved that problem for me by allowing me to minister in jails and prisons for the next 30 years. Nonetheless, it seemed to me that my ministry was limited, and there were times when I was very frustrated about it. One specific day, I said, 'Lord, I don't understand why You would invest so much wisdom and knowledge in me, and not give me an opportunity to talk about it with anybody else outside of the prison ministry."

At the time I was endeavoring to be physically healthy. I was running six miles a day for two or three days a week. A bridge crosses the Dan River close to our home in the country. On the other side of the bridge is the small community of Milton, North Carolina. One of those days when I was meditating on my lack of opportunity for ministry, a car stopped at the end of the bridge, and a man got out and walked toward me as I was jogging.

He said, "My life is a mess. I have been trapped by alcoholism for many years. I need help. Is there any way that you can help me?"

I had never seen this man before in my life. To the best of my knowledge, he may have seen me on other days when I ran along the road. Here was the opportunity for me to share something of the knowledge of God. I counseled with him and prayed with him. I learned about the circumstances in his family and befriended him in a way that had results later in my life. After all, he was a neighbor, and

W. Stephen Keel

I was in a position to love my neighbor. When our meeting was over, the Lord spoke to me and said, "My arm is not shortened. I can give you ministry anytime, anywhere I choose. I ask you to wait on Me."

I embraced my role as a "full gospel businessman" on the streets of life. (As a young Christian, I had attended meetings of an organization named Full Gospel Businessman, but that is not what I am talking about.) I saw early in my Christian life that Stephen in the Book of Acts had been a full gospel businessman two thousand years earlier. He walked in the power of God. I received that I, Stephen Keel, could have what Stephen had then. I rested in my role as a businessman who pursues God and looks for opportunities to share his faith. Having entered into that rest, I frequently found myself on airplanes seated next to someone in need of hearing the Gospel. I will say more about that later.

Because I have a background as an airplane pilot, I am a bit sensitive to the mechanical aspects of the airplanes in which I travel. For instance, watching raw fuel leak from an aged plane prior to take off in Haiti seemed to require more tolerance from me than from the other passengers. Once, flying into Lubbock, Texas, the pilot lowered the flaps and the landing gear. Unknown to me, this specific plane was subject to a high degree of vibration when the flaps and gear went down together. The plane shuddered terribly, and I was confident we had a severe mechanical problem. We were about to crash! I was completely convinced that death was imminent!

My first response was to be concerned over my family....my small children. Immediately, I prayed, "Lord, You have cared for us up to this point, and I know that You can care for my family from here on. I commit my wife and my children to You in the name of Jesus. Thank You for caring for them."

The very next thought that came into my mind was about the people on the plane who were about to die. I was sure that many of them did not know the Lord and would be going straight to hell. I immediately started praying for them, "Jesus, be kind and merciful to these people."

Within moments of beginning that prayer, I realized that we weren't going to crash. The plane shuddered less, and suddenly as a pilot, I

He Inclined His Ear

realized that this was a typical mechanical behavior for this kind of plane.

Why did that happened? I believed that it happened because God inclined His ear unto me when I prayed. He was interested in revealing my heart too, not just to Him, but to me. It was a spiritual test. It show me my attitude toward the hereafter....my confidence in His saving grace and the heart He had placed in me for the lost.

W. Stephen Keel

Chapter 4: Escape from Christianity

When I married at 22 years of age, I was of the opinion that bringing children into this world was a huge mistake. My world view was created by philosophies that I had made part of my life. At age 28, my world view was dramatically changed by an encounter with the person the Jesus Christ. Today (2008) I have eight children and two grandchildren. My life has been and is so full that I can harmonize with what David wrote in Psalm 16:11, "Thou hast shown me the path of life. In thy presence is fullness of joy. At thy right hand, there are pleasures forevermore."

It is my hope that those who read about my direct interactions with the living Savior might also have their world view changed. The testimony in the hymn "Amazing Grace" is my testimony. "I once was lost and now I am found. I was blind and now I see." Because I experienced a dramatic revolution in my world view, becoming conscious of how lost I was, I have a deep interest in sharing this good news with other people who are lost.

Nonetheless, these stories about the voice of God are not directed only to the lost. I refer to "Escape from Christianity" (an earlier book I wrote) because many people in the church today are not experiencing the joy of their salvation. They are living lives of duty and performance, seeking to achieve what's expected of them by their peers, their pastor and their culture. A better title would be "Fleeing Cultural Christianity; Experiencing Real Christianity." Besides containing too many words, this accurate title would not have the same shock value.

Not long ago I had this insight. Acknowledged rebellious sinners are often better off than certain miserable members of Christian organizations. It came to me that there is such a thing as being "lost", and there is such a thing as being "profoundly lost". A prostitute, a drug addict, a bank robber, and people in overt sin know that they are lost. Well, that is preferable to being a church member who is living in misery, thinking he is saved by his church membership when he is not! I refer to these people as the "profoundly lost." They haven't

He Inclined His Ear

any hope or sense that things are going to change and that life will get any better. This book is written to both the "lost" and to the "profoundly lost". Both can discover the joy of hearing the voice of God and obeying it. They can find out how truly interested Jesus is in the affairs of their lives.

Several years ago, I watched a well-known religious leader make, what I considered to be, a spectacle of himself. He was on TV praying for some sick person. Periodically he would stop, take a step forward, turn and look upward and say, "Okay, Lord. I know now that is what You want me to do. I will stop praying this way, and I will start praying that way. Is that right? Thank you."

Then he returned to his ministering to that person for a moment. Again, he stopped and looked upward and said, "Oh, yes, Lord. I apologize. I didn't hear You clearly. I will change what I am doing." Then he went back to ministering to that person.

That activity has a lot to do with the subject of this book. For me it was a spectacle. I honestly don't believe that the man was hearing from God the way he was pretending to hear from God. Now you may say, "Well, you are a proponent for hearing the voice of God, and then you criticize someone who is claiming to hear the voice of God."

Well, yes, I am, because there are many voices. Jesus himself made that declaration. I have brought up this controversy to mention that you do not have to take for granted everyone who claims to hear from God. You do not have to assume that everything being spoken is God speaking to you.

What I really prefer to talk about is replacing the 'spectacle' with the 'spectacular'. The possibility of really hearing the voice of God and having Him incline His ear unto us, can and should affect the major issues of our lives. We can discover where to live and what jobs to pursue. We can experience deep physical and emotional healings. Even in the mundane hidden corners of our lives, it is extremely profitable to discover the <u>exciting</u> experience of "His inclined ear".

W. Stephen Keel
Escape from Christianity Continued

I am of the opinion that my freedom and liberty to hear the voice of God and to experience His hand exist in part because of the 12 years I spent totally separated from Christianity. From age 16 to age 28, I went into a church building three times; twice for the weddings of my two sisters and the other time was to desecrate a building in a drunken spree with college friends. I lived totally outside of the Christian tradition. Having now become part of the Christian tradition, it seems evident to me that there is a significant amount of "anti-faith" in the body of Christ. We have heard of gravity and of anti-gravity.

I believe that I have experienced a significant amount of freedom in Christ by coming to Christ, free from the baggage of religious tradition that fuels the "anti-faith" movement. My conviction regarding this has been reinforced as I have ministered the Gospel to men in prison. I discovered that individuals who had not been programmed by any church experiences to "be careful" regarding the "hearing of voices", have been quite eager and willing to allow the Lord to speak to them and through them. This freedom can sometimes result in mass confusion, particularly when there is a lack of grounding in the basic principles taught in the Bible.

I compare this apparent weakness to that of a child learning to walk. One seldom learns to walk without falling down. Many learning to ride bicycles or to roller skate receive some significant wounds. These falls and wounds are a normal and a natural part of growing up. The confusion that I have referred to is likewise normal and natural. In Hebrews chapter 5, at the end of the chapter, we are taught that it is by "experience" they learn to know the difference between good and evil.

With anti-gravity, you are supposed to float along unconnected to the earth. I have encountered many people who are exercising what I call "anti-faith". Their Christian experience is dominated by fear and intimidation. They are unwilling to allow God to speak to them because they don't want to be labeled as weird or be accused of being outside of the "sound" Christian traditions they have cherished.

I am in no way in denial of the fact that there are remarkable testimonies from people who grew up within Christian traditions who have

He Inclined His Ear

had their world view changed by Christ. I praise the Lord for the children of Godly parents who have raised their children in the fear and the admonition of the Lord. I have longed to be counted among that throng. Nonetheless, there is a pseudo church that makes a mockery of biblical Christianity. Many who in times past followed "another Jesus" have now overcome their "anti-faith" and come into a vibrant relationship with Christ. I learned this from another man's testimony; a man who is no longer with us and whom I will not name, but who has a remarkable testimony.

He told this story at a Baptist church in a rural community where many were living in a state of "anti-faith". He began his testimony by saying, "I know who you are. I am you. I have lived most of my life in a church identical to this one. I was the deacon of deacons. I spent 30 years singing the same hymns that you sing, sitting in the same kind of pews you have, but I had a rather remarkable occurrence.

"Even though I was deeply involved in the church, I really did not know Jesus. There were many things in my life that didn't please Him. For instance, I owned a liquor store. I owned a motel. My best customers at the motel were people who were living in adulterous relationships. I didn't have any compunction about it. My conscience wasn't provoked by either of these circumstances. In actuality, I was one of my own best customers at the liquor store. I drank more and more, and I lived in deep contradiction to what the Bible teaches. I decided that I was going to end it all. I drank turpentine. Drinking turpentine results in your lungs filling up with fluid. This almost instantly brings on pneumonia and kills you very rapidly.

"At 52 years of age, I was in a coma in a hospital bed surrounded by my family and doctors. I could hear them talking, even though I was unconscious. The doctor was explaining to my family that I would not live through the night and that they should put my affairs in order. As they were talking, I looked at the foot of my bed and I saw Jesus. He was standing there looking at me. His face was shining and full of love. He reached out and touched my foot at the end of the bed, and I instantly woke up and said, 'I have seen the Lord!'

"He has healed me!

W. Stephen Keel

"The doctor and my family members were shocked by what had occurred. I got out of the bed at that moment, put my clothes on and left the hospital. The first things I did was sell the motel and close the liquor store. The Lord is leading me now in such an incredible way. I just came back from Nepal, where I was telling people there about Jesus. I have had such an exciting life since I saw Jesus. I want you people to know that you can come alive in Jesus, too."

A skeptics response to this story would be to dismiss his experience of "seeing the Lord" as a hallucination. It might even be possible to suggest that the cancellation of the death pronouncement was fortunate, but not significant. What is significant is that a life that had been lived in self-worship and that was on the brink of self-destruction was changed. The end-result was 20 years of caring for others and a zeal for communicating the Gospel of Jesus Christ.

If your life is cold, you are living in "anti-faith". If fear and tradition are controlling your life, it doesn't have to be that way. You too can come alive in Christ by receiving a vision of the God who inclines His ear unto you.

The Calling of a Spiritual Mid-wife

At one point Jesus said, "According to your faith, be it unto you."

I believe that your reading of these stories can create faith in the same way that faith was created in my life. What is it we are willing to believe for? How earnestly will we approach the throne room of heaven?

In 1974, I had an airplane that had recently been repaired in New York State. I have an anointing for wrecking airplanes too. Nancy and I had rebuilt it, but we had not done a very good job. We turned it over to a mechanic in New York to make the repairs on our repairs. This took several months. We were living in Virginia having a wonderful time discovering the newness of life in Christ. We lived in the Harrisonburg, Virginia area. The time came when I needed to go to New York to retrieve my plane. My father was a student pilot, and he had been flying the plane, but it was my plane, and I wanted to go to get it back.

He Inclined His Ear

If I drove up, I would have the cost of gas and the problem of bringing the car back when I brought the airplane back so I made the decision to hitchhike to Syracuse, New York from Harrisonburg, Virginia. In those days, people hitchhiked far more often than they do today. I stood on the shoulder of Interstate 81 and began holding out my thumb.

I was not financially constrained. I didn't actually have to hitchhike, but I felt that it was what God wanted me to do, and I wanted to do it. I wanted to see the hand of God function in my life. As I stood there, I had an intense conversation with the Lord.

I said, "Lord, there are a lot of cars on this road, and it seems reasonable to me that I might be able to get rides from here to New York, but I don't want to waste Your time or my time to simply save money on car gas. Would You please, in the name of Jesus, do this for me? Would You have only people that are interested in becoming Christians stop and pick me up? You know what I am talking about. There are some people that You are drawing, and they are right on the cusp of receiving You. They need somebody to give them a little bit of information and to offer an opportunity to pray with them to receive You as their Lord and Savior. So, Lord, here is what I propose to do. I would rather continue standing here and not get any rides at all, than have just anybody pick me up. I am asking You in the name of Jesus; please don't have anybody pick me up, unless they are someone that You are working with who needs salvation. Alleluia!"

Having prayed that, I stood there for an hour and a half. A lot of cars went by, and I told the Lord that I was happy to know that He was honoring my prayer and that He was not thinking of having any of these cars stop because He has somebody that really, really wants to get saved, and that the person is going to pick me up! Finally a car stopped. When we got underway, I said, "Gee, what's going on in your life?"

He said, "Well, I was just at a Christian music festival. I don't know much about Christianity, but those people were having a really good time. It was an outside event, and we were sitting on the side of a hill. In front of me were two young girls on a blanket who were really getting into the music. They were smiling, actually glowing and having a wonderful time. I don't have any idea in the world what was going on, but I would sure like to know what it is that these people have that makes them so happy."

I said, "Well, let me tell you about Jesus. Let me tell you why they are so happy."

I began to preach the Gospel to him, but I didn't take a lot of time or give him unnecessary information. He was clearly an answer to my prayer. He was ready to get saved. So I said, "Would you like to have what they have?"

He said, "Yes, I would."

I said, "Why don't you pull over on the shoulder and let me help you pray. I will lead you in a prayer of salvation so that you can become a Christian."

He said, "Yeah, that's a great idea!"

He pulled over on the side of Interstate 81 and we prayed. As we drove on, we talked further, increasing his excitement in God. Soon he announced that this was as far as he was going, and I would need to get off. He thanked me very much for telling him about Jesus.

I rejoiced! I said, "Lord, how exciting it is that You have heard my prayer. You inclined Your ear unto me. I can hardly believe it. This is wonderful. Who else wants to get saved, Lord? I am anxious to be in Your will."

I stood there for about five minutes this time and another car stopped. Lo and behold, it was a second person eager for salvation. The difference was that this young man had been around even more Christians. We stopped the car a little further up the road in Maryland, and I prayed with him to receive salvation. Then I laid hands on him, and he received the gift of speaking in tongues. He was baptized in the Holy Spirit on the shoulder of Interstate 81. I was rather amazed by the whole thing. I had in my hands a new Bible for which I had paid about $50. That was a lot of money to me, but I felt that it was the leading of God to give it to him. I said, "Here, you are going to need this."

He Inclined His Ear

I gave him my new Thompson Chain Reference Bible. He drove off and I said, "Okay Lord, who is next?"

It was about a 10-hour ride to the Syracuse, New York area. The seventh person who picked me up was the only one I didn't pray with to receive the Lord. Six people received the Lord between Virginia and New York. The seventh was a young man, a student at Cornell University. He was the intellectual type, and I spent more time with him than anybody else. I challenged him regarding his relationship to Christ. I have to believe that sometime after we talked, he too was able to bow his knee to the Lord Jesus Christ. Only believe!

What are you willing to have faith for? How long will you stand on the side of the road without a ride because you are convinced that you have heard the voice of God, and that He has a purpose for you, and that He is ready to manifest that purpose through you?

The experience that I just shared had another benefit. It developed in my heart a theological position that would be of great value to me in the years to come. Some people have said that I have the anointing of an evangelist. That may be true. I know that the Lord has given me the opportunity to pray with hundreds of people individually to receive Jesus Christ as their Lord and Savior. Why would He have me pray with them? You see, on that trip to New York, I was given an insight. I was shown that I was a spiritual mid-wife. What a mid-wife does is arrive at the time of delivery and assist in the birth.

It is clear to me that no man comes to the Father unless Jesus draws him, and that men are born again, not of the will of man, but of the will of the Father. So, if it is not of the will of the man, then my will as an evangelist is somewhat worthless, but my skill as a mid-wife is very valuable. The Lord revealed to me, that as a Spiritual mid-wife, my most significant role is to have my spiritual eyes open continually. I am required to discern who is full term and in labor. If I would do that, I would be positioned to bring people into the kingdom. He continues sending people my way today who are ready to get saved. How often it has occurred, I can't count. My responsibly is to be conscious of what the Lord is doing. The really big benefit of this is the understanding that I cannot fail, because I AM NOT THE ONE WHO IS DOING THE SAVING.

W. Stephen Keel

I recall a particular trip to St. Louis on a commercial airplane where a lady sat next to me. She was in a terrible state of mind. She had gotten up at 4am that morning and driven to the airport only to miss her flight. She then had to drive another two hours to another airport. What should have been a relatively simple trip, took her eight hours of frustration before being seated on a plane headed for St. Louis.

I told her that Jesus was the Lord of everything, including her eight hour trial. Before we landed in St. Louis, she bowed her knee to the Savior and acknowledged Jesus Christ as Lord, entering into the joy of the Lord. As she got off the plane, she exclaimed, "It was such a wonderful thing that I missed the first flight." She knew that if she had gotten on the other plane, she would have missed meeting me and not had the opportunity to pray to receive Jesus!

Hold My Tongue, O God

Hearing from God and experiencing God doesn't always have to occur in the realm of great difficulty or need. The Lord can also manifest Himself simply to delight us, to prove a point, and to show how much He delights in interacting with us. For a season of our lives, we lived in Roswell, New Mexico, where I pursued my career in the wind energy industry. I had a business manufacturing a device called a kite anemometer. It was used for site selection of wind energy conversion systems in 20 countries around the world.

Our stay in New Mexico was not merely a business opportunity. God placed my family and me there to teach us many things. In fact, I had had a bad experience with a church group that I had been part of for seven years in Virginia. The congregation where I had enjoyed my "first love" in Christ had experienced a great upheaval. I may or may not write about that story. I was very happy to get away and to live in New Mexico.

One of the things we did while we were in Roswell, was to study the "church". We visited 28 churches in one and a half years. I was on a crusade to discover "truth" about the universal church of Jesus Christ. I talked to the pastors, the elders and the Sunday school teachers. My wife and I took a class at the Roman Catholic Church to see first-hand

He Inclined His Ear

what they taught and believed. When we attended the church, they assumed we were Roman Catholic because we had so many children.

One Sunday, the conservative Lutheran minister taught that the reason J.F. Kennedy had been shot was that the church had not been praying for the country's leaders according to the instructions found in the New Testament. The following Tuesday morning at 10am, I was thinking about what he had said. I stopped my work and prayed for the then President Ronald Reagan. Only minutes later I learned that the president had been shot, but that it was not fatal.

Pastors of conservative Missouri Synod Lutheran Churches are not known for claiming the ability to prophesy in the Spirit. When I heard that President Reagan had been shot, it occurred to me that the pastor had spoken as Caiaphas the high priest, not knowing that he was prophesying. I decided to tell the pastor about all of this the following Sunday morning.

The Missouri Synod Church has a hymn book that contains the liturgy of the various services that are to be conducted during the liturgical calendar. It also has lists of Scripture lessons that are to be read on dated Sundays for many years in advance. Using King James words to describe the situation, "lo and behold," the Scripture assigned for reading on that Sunday was the very scripture that mentions Caiaphas prophesying when he was not aware of the fact that he was prophesying. These events and these details further convinced me that the Lord is intimately involved in the lives of all men everywhere.

The purpose for visiting all of these churches was simply to understand God. I was grappling with obtaining knowledge of God and at the same time reading a lot of church history. We were so deeply involved in the process that on a particular Sunday, we visited three different congregations in the same day. This produced an interesting insight into the role of the Holy Spirit's teaching. The three congregations were totally unrelated to each other. They were associated with three different denominations. In each of these three meetings, we received a message focused on II Thessalonians, chapter 4. Either this was a divine coincidence, or the Holy Spirit was teaching on this subject. Perhaps a statistician could extrapolate from our experience the number of churches worldwide that were focused on the same subject on that particular Sunday.

The overall conclusion of our visits to these many congregations influenced the direction of our lives for years to come. We discovered that church theological persuasions made very little impact on the character or quality of spiritual experience of the various members of the various churches. People were the same in every congregation. No one ever seemed to feel required to bring up the issues that separated themselves from the other churches. The intensity of prayer and the focus in worship may have been slightly higher or lower, depending on the practice of the particular congregation, but the people themselves were indistinguishable from each other. We discovered that in every congregation, there was a core group of more zealous believers who fellowshipped together. Based on the general apathy toward God which we found in most church people, it is possible that these core groups are the literal "life" of churches everywhere. This observation led us to seek out the "core" believers wherever we went.

One of the organizations that we visited was the Full Gospel Businessmen's Association of Roswell. We had been invited to the home of one of its leaders who had invited a nationally, well-known man of God named Ben Kinchlow to speak at their meeting. Ben was associated with Pat Robertson at CBN at that time. He travelled and spoke to Full Gospel Businessmen's Associations across the United States. It was a great honor for this small chapter to have him as their speaker. After the event, we were invited to one of the leader's home for a reception to meet Ben Kinchlow personally. It was held in a palatial Spanish hacienda.

My wife and I realized that I have put my "foot in my mouth" many times in the past. We had a conversation about this as we drove through the desert looking forward to the evening. We decided that it probably wouldn't be a good thing for me to be too outspoken or say things that were controversial. We prayed and asked the Lord to control my tongue and to be the Lord over what I would say and over what I wouldn't say. That's a good prayer.

When we got to the reception; chance, serendipity or whatever you want to call it (God's providence) found me in line standing next to

He Inclined His Ear

Ben Kinchlow. It is interesting that when people have national prominence, other people feel uncomfortable around them. It was clear to me that no one in the line felt comfortable to carry on a conversation with him. Long ago, the Lord had removed fear of man from my heart, so I thought maybe he needed someone to chat with. I introduced myself and began to converse with him about his childhood and listen to him tell some stories about his life. I told him some of my own. We filled our plates at the buffet and separated to eat at our respective tables.

After eating, I began exploring the large home of our host. There were guest milling about in many of the finely decorated rooms. Our host was in the oil business and had done oil explorations in Israel in the hope that it would provide oil and revenues for that nation's needs. I walked past the door to his study and saw Ben and another man chatting. Because of my previous talk with Ben, I felt comfortable enough to step into the room, greet them and talk. Seeking common ground for the conversation, I mentioned that I had seen Ben and Pat Robertson interview a lady who was promoting a product referred to as Ezekiel Bread. (It is worth noting that this may have been one of five "700 Club" programs that I have watched in my entire life.)

The recipe for Ezekiel Bread was something that God had given this lady. She had had it tested and discovered that it was a perfect food. If people would eat it, they would be healthy. It had a long shelf life, and in the event that Christians were not raptured and had to endure the tribulation period, this would be the perfect food for survival.

I said to Ben, "I would like to know about the lady with the Ezekiel Bread. I am interested because I happened to be in Washington, DC, in my patent attorney's office when he received a phone call from her. My attorney told her that patents and copyrights are intended for new ideas that have not been publically disclosed, and that if this recipe comes from information that is in the Bible, she may not be able to patent it. That ended the conversation, but she persisted, and she achieved a patent on her recipe somehow for Ezekiel Bread. My attorney told me that she had reached some agreement with Arrowhead Mills and that they were going to start selling the product through their manufacturing facility."

Ben said, "Well, it is interesting that you should bring that up, but I don't think that I am the one you should talk to about it. You need to talk to the president of Arrowhead Mills."

He turned to the man standing beside him and introduced me.

I was about speechless. I said, "Oh!"

That man said, "Regarding manufacturing her bread, we won't be doing that. The contract negotiations fell through late last week. The patent holder was demanding a dominate role in both the sales and manufacturing going beyond our expected relationship with the "inventor." She would have effectively had total control of that product and we were not willing to enter that agreement. But I have heard that she has is negotiating a contract with another bread distributor."

This conversation was quite provocative because we had prayed that I would control my tongue and say only the things I was supposed to say and not say what I was not supposed to say. I stepped out of the room in a bit of shock with a desire to find my wife to tell her of the amazing coincidence of apparently putting my foot in my mouth.

I found Nancy and one other guest in the adjacent room. I walked up to her and said, "Honey, the most unusual thing just happened. You know how we prayed that God would let me say certain things and not let me say certain things?"

I told her the story of what had just happened; about how I had talked to Ben Kinchlow about Arrowhead Mills. I told her how the president of Arrowhead Mills was standing right there listening to me and wasn't that amazing? And then I told how the Ezekiel Bread deal had fallen through because they were having a problem with what appeared to be a controlling personality. When I finished, the gentleman who had been talking to my wife said that this was a very interesting story. Then he introduced himself. He was Mr. So-and-so, the president of the other distribution company that was in contract negotiations for the bread recipe!

Well, the night still wasn't over. I had the opportunity to speak prophetically into another life. I conversed with a man who was a redeemed homosexual. He had questions about sharing his testimony. I explained to him that the HIDDEN works of darkness were the only

He Inclined His Ear

things that were a danger to him, and if he would proclaim that he was not ashamed of the salvation of God, and that he had been delivered from homosexuality, then the devil would not be able to ensnare him again. You might agree with this counsel or not agree with it, but I received unction from the Lord, especially in the light of my earlier conversation and my prayer that the Lord would control my tongue.

W. Stephen Keel

Chapter 5: I Talk, He Listens, Things Happen

Every man and woman of God who has their heart fine-tuned by the Holy Spirit experiences trials and difficulties. The Scripture shows us clearly that we can rejoice when we encounter various trials, because these trials bear patience and patience bears perfection. Even though we read it in the Bible, we are not eager to embrace difficulties, especially when they linger, lasting months or even years.

A young man raising a family wants to provide for them financially. His sense of self-worth is tied to his success. The Lord chose to show me that He is the source of our provision. The way He chose to show me this was by allowing my work to be unprofitable.

I had a season of success manufacturing and selling a product called a kite anemometer. I could measure the tension on the kite string and discover the speed of the wind any place at any altitude. The kite was a scientifically proven instrument. I sold various models to research teams in twenty-five countries. People in both the wind energy and air pollution industry discovered the value in the Tethered Aerodynamically Lifting Anemometer (TALA).

As it happens, times changed. The price of oil went below $11 a barrel, the break-even number for sustaining the viability of wind energy. Attitudes toward alternate energy changed, and tax credits disappeared. These circumstances correctly predicted that the kite anemometer business would not continue to prosper.

We were still living in Roswell, New Mexico at the time. The kite used in our product line had been designed by Ray Holland, an aeronautical engineer from Roswell. That season of life had been very pleasant. We had diligently sought the face of God. We had moved to Roswell for business reasons and to "experience the church". Just before we moved, our church in Virginia had suffered a disaster. Our pastor had failed morally. The congregation was in pain, and we were happy to be called away.

While living in Roswell, I purposefully sought out the matter of "church." Having been in a bad church situation, I wanted to know what church was all about. I determined to investigate the issue. We didn't do it haphazardly. We did it intensely. I talked at length with lay people, pastors, elders and Sunday school teachers about their understanding of their church experience. One Sunday, I asked about the denial of the trinity and the virgin birth that were published in the preface to a new hymn book, recently purchased by a particular congregation. A mature church member was unable to answer my question. He had never read the preface of the hymnal and acted surprised at its statement of unbelief.

I say again that I could tell very little difference between the Pentecostals, the Fundamentalists and the Evangelicals. Their lives appeared to be very, very similar.

Throughout the years to come, that observation continued to hold true. And, additionally we could always find fellowship with zealous Christians if we looked for them. Home church in the latter years proved to be the most fulfilling for ourselves and for the families we met with.

Seeing the wind energy business come to a standstill in 1981, I needed to hear from the Lord about what to do and where to live next. While traveling to visit a customer and a vendor on a wind energy project in Denver, I had a serious conversation with the Lord.

I said, "Lord, it is clear to me that the tax credits are drying up, and the price of oil is going down, and the wind energy business is going to change dramatically. Even though I have this opportunity right now, I won't be able to make a living in this business in the near future. I'm in Roswell because of the business, but I am confident that You have a move in store for us, and You are prompting me to ask where it is You want us to move. I am asking You, where in the world would You have my wife, family and me to go?"

Almost immediately I got a response. I heard or it was impressed upon my mind as the following: "Please describe to Me what you would like to have in a home and the nature of the community you would like to live in."

I didn't expect God to give me a shopping list, but I thought about it.

I said, "I would like it to be a place in the country, a spacious place with plenty of bedrooms for all my children. Because I fly airplanes, I would like an airport not too far away. I would like a climate that is not very hot and not very cold, where trees grew. Roswell is in a desert and I missed the trees."

As I was making these responses, I heard the voice of the Lord say, "You already own that house."

When I heard that, I was distraught, because a year and a half previously, we had moved out of our home in Ringgold, Virginia, precisely because of the turmoil and problems within the church. When I turned my back on that house, I turned my back on that house forever. I had no intention of ever returning to the community of confusion that we had left behind. Curiously, the house had been on the market all that time. It was a beautiful home on top of a hill with a gorgeous view, but not a single perspective buyer came to look at the house. The realtor couldn't find anyone interested in buying our home. That was significant to me.

Realizing no one would buy it and realizing that the house fit the description that the Lord had asked me to give, I said, "Alright Lord, although it breaks my heart, and although I have no desire or interest in returning to that community, I can see clearly that You have ordained for me and my family to move back to that house, so I submit to it now."

As I submitted, I experienced a spiritual and an emotional breaking of my heart.

Although I am characteristically an optimist, upbeat sort of person, at that moment I was not exactly discouraged, but I was profoundly broken. I offered one more prayer: I said, "Lord, there have been many times when I have ridden on airplanes that You have caused someone to sit next to me that needed to hear from You, and You caused me to be the person who brought to them comfort and good news. I don't know how You are going to do it, but I know that I am broken and in need of comfort myself. I ask You, in the name of Jesus, would You send someone to comfort me. Thank You, Lord."

He Inclined His Ear

The plane landed in the Denver airport. I took a seat where the luggage carousels were. I remember clearly that these huge airplanes would land having as many as 400 people on them. Suddenly 400 people would go by me and then no one and then another flood of 400 people. I sat there reading the New Testament when an individual came and sat next to me. I saw only his foot and a leg in green army uniform. Immediately, the voice of God said, "This is the answer to your prayer. This is the person I have sent to comfort you."

The next thing I heard was the strong voice of a Lt. Colonel say to me, "That's a great Book you are reading."

I said, "Amen, brother!" and we engaged in a conversation. He told me he had come from Florida where he had attended "Evangelism Explosion," a conference that taught personal evangelism to men who were not clergymen but could be used of the Lord to win souls to Christ. Based on what I have written earlier about not becoming a professional preacher, you can see how close that was to my heart. My conversation with this good brother was a distinct comfort.

Later that day when I arrived in Portland, I discovered that the vendor I was working with was in a peculiar "religious" position. We returned from our meetings to the hotel that night, and he began to tell me his story. He said that on the previous day, he had received final notification from the Mormon Church that he was no longer a Mormon. He said that he had resigned from the Mormon Church.

I said, 'That is very interesting. Why did you do that?"

He explained that as a business person, he travelled quite a bit, and when he traveled, it was convenient to meet women for sex. He was enjoying his sexual relationships outside of marriage, but when he came home to be with his wife and especially when he was around the church, he experienced a tremendous sense of guilt. He had decided that he didn't want to give up the women, so he thought it appropriate to resign from the church.

He didn't understand at the time that it would be as complicated as it was. He learned that he had to go through a period of "withdrawal" during which the church leaders went through the genealogical records. He was a multi-generational Mormon. They went through the records and unraveled the consequences of his leaving, relative to the various positions in heaven of people related to him. After several months, they announced they had accomplished the task, so they could officially declare that he was no longer a Mormon.

They had two important pieces of information they needed to explain to him, which were explained to him the day before we talked. He was told that the leaders of the church were confident that, due to his upbringing, he would want to continue contributing money to the church. He could still do that, but it wouldn't be possible to give directly to the church. He would need to give his money to his cousin or a member in good standing who could, in turn, give the money to the church. Secondly, he had it explained to him that undoubtedly he would like to be present for church services now and then because it was such an important part of his life. He could still do that, but since he was no longer a Mormon, it would not be permissible for him to pray while he was in the church building.

As he shared these consequences of his actions, I knew that this man really needed to know something more about Jesus. I said, "Maybe some of the problem with your guilt in the church is related to the fact that you don't have a good grasp of who Jesus Christ is, and what He wants to do in your life. Jesus wants to have a walking, talking relationship with you, and He wants to give you the desires of your heart. He can take away the desire for the women and replace it with a desire for godliness. Let me illustrate to you how much Jesus wants to talk to you and walk with you. You see, this morning when I left Roswell, I realized that the wind energy business was going to dry up, and I would have to move.

I told him the whole story. I told him how I had asked the Lord to send someone to comfort me and that the Lord had set a man next to me and told me that that was the answer to my prayer.

I don't know the ultimate outcome of telling that story to this disaffected Mormon, but I know that he heard something that was significant. It was significant to me and it was significant to him.

He Inclined His Ear

Man Plans, But God Executes

When my children were considerably younger, I was struggling financially. I had been an entrepreneur and worked a number of years with a moderate amount of success. In a particular season of my life, I found myself quite unsuccessful. I had a lot of responsibility, and I needed an income to supply the needs of my family. At that time we owned a milk cow. I was committed to milking the cow every morning and every night. It was a great blessing because it provided enough milk for our family and for several families in the community. Knowing my financial need, a brother in the Lord invited me to travel to Nags Head, North Carolina to work with him. He was earning a substantial amount of money hanging sheetrock in condominiums and beachfront houses. He told me that, if I could come, he could give me work, and I could earn hundreds of dollars in a short period of time.

After praying about it, I made the decision to hitchhike to Nags Head from our home near Danville, Virginia. It is about a six-hour drive. The reason for hitchhiking was to save money on gas and to leave my wife a vehicle to drive while I was gone. I made arrangements for someone to milk the cow, and I had my wife drop me off near Roxboro, North Carolina on Highway 158.

Nancy dropped me off in the country on the highway that was a direct route to Nags Head. I felt that I would have a good chance to find someone going all the way along that road. Ten o'clock in the morning seemed to be a good time for getting where I was going. Confident that I was doing the right thing, I proceeded to seek the Lord in prayer and worship as I waited on the roadside. I worshipped and I sang and I prayed. The weather was warm and comfortable. I was basically having a good time, but I noticed that there was not much traffic.

I had made a quality decision to offer the sacrifice of praise no matter what, so I continued to worship and sing and pray, but time was passing by. Before I knew it, I had been standing there for four hours, what seemed to me to be an extraordinary amount of time. I realized that I probably wouldn't get to Nags Head that day and that I could find myself standing on the road at night in the wintertime. I began to earnestly pray, questioning if I was intended to go on this trip at all!

As men would do, I assessed the value of going and compared it with the consequences of staying home. I considered my ways. This process took about another hour of time, and now I had been standing in the same spot for five hours! Not a single car had even slowed down to pick me I up.

In the book of Proverbs, it teaches that man casts the lot, but God decides how the lot falls, so it occurred to me, having seen others do something similar, that I would cast a lot to discover whether or not I should continue on my trip. This was before the days of the cell phones, so there was no way to contact my wife to get her opinion. It was just God and me.

I cast the lot, and the decision was to turn around and go home. I stepped across this small country highway and turned to face toward home. In less than a minute a vehicle came along and stopped. The young driver offered me a ride. I was utterly amazed that I had stood for five hours going in one direction having no "luck", but as soon as I turned to go in the other direction by the cast of the lot, I was picked up in less than a minute! Being provoked by the apparent evidence that God was the Author of the event, I immediately questioned the young man driving the car about his relationship with God.

He said, "It is interesting that you should ask because last night I was at a church meeting near Durham, and I responded to an altar call. I asked Jesus Christ to become Lord and Savior of my life. That was a huge turn of events for me, but today I really don't understand what's happening in my life. I am just in the car driving around trying to figure things out." Durham was about 30 minutes away from where he had picked me up, and where I lived was another 45 minutes north.

I said, "If you are just driving about, is there any possibility that you could give me a ride home? This would give me an opportunity to answer some of the questions you have on your heart."

He said, "Sure, I have nothing else to do. Let's go!" Over the next few hours, including supper at my house, I had the opportunity to disciple this young man and to point him toward the path of righteousness. He left my house about 11pm that night filled to the brim with excitement about his new life in Christ. About a year later, I heard a knock on the door. It was this young man. He said, "I

He Inclined His Ear

thought you would like to know I am still following Jesus and its great!"

Hearing My Name at the Office Supply Store

Fear not, for I have redeemed you. I have called you by your name....
When you walk through the fire, you shall not be burned.
Isaiah 43:1-2

In the Book of Isaiah, the Spirit of God speaks through Isaiah to declare, "Fear not, I have redeemed thee. I have called thee by thy name. Thou art Mine."

That sounds like a theistic God to me, the One that called us by our name. He goes on to say that when you walk through the fire, you shall not be burned, and when you pass through the water, you won't drown. The Scripture records a God who knows us by our name and plucks us out of the fire.

Shadrach, Meshach and Abednego were in a literal fire, and there was a fourth man like unto the Son of God standing alongside of them. When they came out of the fire, they didn't smell of smoke. One might consider that to be a poetic metaphor, or maybe it actually happened. As for me and my house, I am content that God knows me by my name and that He plucks me out of my own personal fires.

My wife Nancy and I were at the office supply store picking up some materials for a booklet that I was attempting to publish. It contained poetry written by men in the maximum custody prison where I ministered. When we left the store, we got in the car and I turned the ignition key. Nothing happened. The starter had failed. We sat there and kind of smiled because the Lord had been working in our lives remarkably in recent days. We were more or less wondering how He was going to get us out of this situation. I had five dollars to my name.

A black man came out of the store and noticed we were not going anywhere. He beckoned me to roll down the window, which I did. He asked if we were having trouble of some sort. I said, "Not really. This is just one of those situations that is creating perfection in our life. You know what it says in James that we are to rejoice when we encounter various trials and tribulations because tribulation bears patience and patience bears perfection. Well, we are being perfected right now. The starter in our car has failed, and I can't get it to work."

Now I had never seen this man before, and he had never seen me before, but he said, "I am a pastor. Maybe I can help you."

I said, "Well, I am a pastor of sorts. I have a rather unusual congregation though. I have one of the most racially mixed congregations in the community. They are all locked up in a maximum custody prison."

He said, "Oh, what is your name?"

I said, "I am Stephen Keel."

He said, "Would you wait for just a minute, please." He stepped away from the car and went to his car that was parked next to us. He reached in the back seat, and he pulled out a Bible. He came back and said, "I am from Greensboro, North Carolina (about an hour away) and I am on my way to Cascade, Virginia (which is about 30 minutes to the north.) I just happened to stop here. I want to show you something."

He said he had been in a meeting last night with the board of deacons in his church. They had decided that they would like to get involved in prison ministry. Someone had asked him how to do that and someone else said that he had heard of this man named Stephen Keel that is working as a chaplain over at Blanch Prison in Blanch, North Carolina.

"So I wrote your name down on this piece of paper," and he opened up his Bible, and he pulled out the paper, and on it was my name Stephen Keel!

The pastor then said, "Why don't you come with me. I think I can help you. I know a mechanic close by."

We went to the mechanic who said he had a friend with a tow truck who could get our car. They got our car and brought it back to the mechanic. He took the starter out. The pastor said he knew a place where the starter could be repaired not very far away. "Let's go over there and get it fixed."

He Inclined His Ear

I am thinking to myself, "I have no money to fix this."

We went to B and B Alternators and Repair Shop. They repaired it while we waited, and they presented us a bill for $40 for the work. The pastor had no way of knowing that my bank account was completely empty. Nancy and I considered writing a check and believing God for the funds.

As we reached for our checkbook, the pastor said, "Oh, no, no, no! Let me take care of this." He paid the $40 to repair the starter. He took us back to the shop with the repaired starter and gave it to the mechanic.

The mechanic put the starter in our car and started it up. Once again I was faced with a bill and I had no way to pay. I pulled out my checkbook again and said let me pay you for this. He said, "Oh, no. I believe God has told me that I am not supposed to charge you for this."

We went home from that experience more fully convinced than ever that God has called us by our name and that He has a purpose for us. At the time, it seemed a waste of several hours in the middle of the day. We had experienced stress that I really didn't want to have to go through, but it was for a purpose to demonstrate how carefully God watches over us. How many events like this have occurred in your life? Are you walking in the obvious interaction with the living God? If not, it may be that although you call yourself a theist, in fact you are practicing deism...believing that God is disconnected from you and far away.

I am hoping that by sharing these stories from a very normal kind of life and having problems that everybody faces on a routine basis, you can be encouraged to change your theology and your practices. You will no longer merely hold to the doctrine of theism but practice it.

How many times have we experienced this sort of thing? I recall the time that we sat in the living room of our home facing the fact that we had a $3000 bill that was due now. That amount in 1988 was a significant amount of money. We had no idea where it was going to come from, so we did what seemed reasonable. We prayed, "Father, You know our need. You have declared in Your Word that You have heard our cry even before we called, and that You will supply our needs according to Your riches in glory in Christ Jesus. So we ask You Lord, in the name of Jesus, please provide for the payment of this bill. Amen."

Brrrrrrrrng! The telephone rang. I went to the phone. "Hello, this is so-and-so, and I need to order such and such item and have it shipped right away." The profit from that sale was exactly $3000!

He Inclined His Ear

Chapter 6: Hearing Can Be About Hearing

I could hear, *then I could hear*. Some Christian friends and I had been ministering on Sunday mornings in a local jail. The Lord had honored the ministry, and many inmates were being converted to Christ. It was really a very exciting time in our lives. On a particular Sunday morning I stood before the people that had gathered for church in the jailhouse. I was playing the guitar and singing a favorite inmate song, "Down at the Cross Where My Savior Died". As we were singing, suddenly a loud ringing erupted in my left ear, and I realized that I had gone deaf in that ear. My first thought was "Lord, how can this be? Have I displeased You in any way? Is there any part of my life that is unsatisfactory to You that has resulted in the removal of the shield of protection around my life? Why should I find myself struck in this way?"

I heard a still small voice say that the reason you have lost your hearing is that you haven't been listening to Me. I said, "What do You mean, Lord?"

In a matter of seconds I received from the still small voice that the entrepreneurial work I had been doing for the previous three months was not in the will of God. The book of Proverbs says, "It's the king's prerogative to discover and invent."

I have been an entrepreneur most of my life. At that particular time, I was working on a concept that now is known on the internet as Auto Trader. The only problem was that the Internet did not exist at the time I was creating this project. I had developed a data base containing information on used automobiles, and I was in the process of developing relationships with automobile dealerships around the country. The idea was I would have the information on used automobiles immediately available. I called it "Fast Finders".

An interesting thing about the project was that I was getting much encouragement from men, but I was not getting any encouragement from God. When I prayed about it, I didn't hear much, but when I talked to various business men, they all said that's a great idea. At one point I even talked to people at the Wharton School of Business in Philadelphia, and they said this was something that could have national impact. I was very encouraged by that.

But, when my hearing evaporated in the meeting, I knew that I had not been listening to the voice of the Spirit. Immediately I said, "I repent. Lord, forgive me. The project is over. I know that I need to obey Your voice more than anything else."

For the next two weeks, I walked about with a profound deafness in my left ear. I went to an audiologist, and I went to an ear, nose and throat specialist. Both confirmed through testing and examination that I had experienced sudden nerve death. That means that the auditory nerve in my ear had died unexpectedly. The surgeon told me that I could spend $2,500 and have an experimental operation. When it was over, I would still be deaf and be out $2,500. The audiologist told me that he sees this case several times a year and that it is irreversible. He said I would learn to accommodate the tinnitus, the loud ringing in my ear. This was not the news I wanted to hear. I had six daughters and one son. My son was 3 years old, and when he walked into the room and spoke, the frequency of his voice was such that it caused my ear to hurt. I had pain in my ear whenever I listened to the voice of my only son. I now knew even better that I needed to listen to the voice of God's only Son.

That was not fun. I couldn't hear or play Christian music anymore because it caused pain and distortion in my ear. I entered into a period of what I refer to as abject faithlessness. I was totally convinced that the doctors were right and that I would never hear in that ear again. I endeavored patiently to endure the pain. Two weeks into the experience of deafness, I received a phone call from a man whom I had known for several years in Christ. This particular man, before his salvation, had been a very committed homosexual. He had been deeply involved in male prostitution. It had affected his manner of speech, his walk, even his facial features. Everything about him confirmed "I am a homosexual," but in his heart, he had received the Lordship of Jesus Christ. He had been delivered from his homosexual lifestyle, but not from the visible effects.

He Inclined His Ear

I was one of a few people that had befriended him and given him an opportunity for Christian fellowship. He was one of the last people I would ever have anticipated as being a "savior" in my life, but two weeks into my deafness, he called me. In my one good ear I heard him say, "Brother Steve, I know about your deafness. I know about your pain, but I have heard from God. The Lord has told me that you have a ministry that will not be held back by deafness, because He is going to deliver you from deafness, and you are going to walk in that ministry. He has also told me that I am supposed to pray for you once, and only once, and when I finish praying, it will be a completed operation, and we will never have to discuss it again except to give God praise and honor for your healing."

I sat listening to his nice words of encouragement, as I wallowed in faithlessness. I could only see in my mind's eye, this rejected hulk of humanity that no one wanted anything to do with. Yet he was making such a profound statement of faith on my behalf. I made a decision in my heart. If this is one of those grains of mustard seed faith that is required, I can offer that grain of mustard seed faith in agreement with my brother. Thank You, Lord. However You want to work in my life, I thank You.

We said good bye and I picked up the phone a second time. I had discovered from the audiologist that the machine that they use to test our hearing was nothing more than a tone generator. I had a touch-tone telephone where I could touch different numbers on the keypad and get different frequencies. Some frequencies were high and some were low. I put the phone to my deaf ear, and I punched the buttons on the keypad. At that very moment, I could hear better in the deaf ear than I could hear in my good ear.

Naturally I was impressed. The pain was gone. The loud ringing was gone. I could understand what people were saying. My hearing had totally returned and it stayed returned. I went back to the audiologist to tell him what had happened.

He said let me test you. After he tested me, he took me into his office. He said, "I am a Christian, but I don't believe in the miracles or the healing ministries that are being promoted on television or anywhere else. It is my opinion that those preachers are charlatans whose only interest is bilking the people out of their money. That's what I believe. If you had come into this office and told me what had happened to you, I would have looked you in the eye and told you that you were a liar. But I tested you before this experience of healing and I have tested you after it. The fact is you can hear better in your deaf ear now than you can hear in your good ear. I have no other recourse but to declare that you have experienced a miracle from God."

Praise the Lord! I already knew that, but it was really good to have him tell me that.

What did I learn from this? Well, I am not the only person that can hear from God. This brother who prayed for me, obviously heard the voice of God. The proof is in the well-being of my ear, which to this day is perfectly well and normal.

I also saw that a portion of the body of Christ often puts guilt and condemnation on people by telling them that the reason they didn't get healed was due to their lack of faith. If they would only believe... how many times have I heard that? Only believe.... Well, in my experience, I received a healing when I didn't believe! That proved to me that the grace of God is truly without merit. It is not based all the time on the strength of our faith.

I exercised a mustard seed of faith, and evidently that mustard seed of faith released the healing, but where did that mustard seed of faith come from? I believe it came from enabling grace. It was a gift from God himself. He planted it there when I didn't have it. When I was bankrupt to my own hurt, He caused another with faith to speak words of faith which stirred faith in me. Faith manifested itself in healing. If it can happen for me, it can happen for you.

The Lord Gives Better than He Takes

The following story will never be turned into a soap opera or a prime time movie. It is too normal and natural. I have included it because I believe that we all can have experiences like this. If we sensitize ourselves to the reality of what is happening, we can be awed by the many times we see the hand of God functioning in our lives. We can live in an attitude of awe.

He Inclined His Ear

In the early 1980's, I was working in the prison ministry. Bryant Hudson and I were led to provide a place to live and work for a young man who was getting out of prison. We wanted to give him an opportunity to re-enter society. He lived with Bryant for about three months. We had no clue of what was about happen next.

On a chilly morning in the fall of the year, my wife and I arose early and were standing in our bedroom talking about the goodness of God. We discussed how He had revealed Himself to us in so many ways. We specifically mentioned the fact that whenever it appeared that Jesus had taken something away from us, He replaced it with something better than that which had been taken. As soon as we mentioned this, I looked out the window from our upstairs bedroom and discovered that our automobile was missing.

I knew immediately that our car had been stolen. The young man that we had been helping was an individual who was "institutionalized" in his mind. He was having trouble dealing with freedom. He wanted to go back to prison, so he chose to steal some tools from my workshop and my automobile to take a trip to California. We did not know the details of the theft until later when the stolen car was returned to the insurance company.

We reported the theft to the police and to our insurance agent. My mother-in-law was quite concerned about even reporting it. She was afraid that we would not receive money from the insurance company because the doors were not locked and the key was in the ignition of the car. She concluded that he didn't really steal it; we more or less gave it to him. We called the insurance company anyhow. We discussed the fact that the keys had been left in the ignition, but that it had been clearly stolen. Within a week of that event, we received a check from the insurance company for $3700.

This was better than I had expected as the previous week I had been looking for another car. I had gone to several car dealers and found the trade-in value for my car. The best offer for my car was $2800, so we considered this check of $3700 to be a fulfillment of what we had been discussing. We had received back something more than what had been taken away. Little did we know that the Lord had something even more interesting in mind.

W. Stephen Keel

I was in the computer business at the time and had a fax machine. In a systematic mindset, I decided to pray first and to ask the Lord to describe to me the specific car I should get to replace the one that was lost. Once I had a clear understanding of it, I could circulate a fax to car dealers in the area describing the car and the money I would pay for it. After praying, I received that due to my growing family, I needed a late model station wagon with a back seat that folded down, with less than 30,000 miles in good mechanical condition. I decided that it was appropriate that I spend no more than $4,000 for the car.

I was confident that this was a simple matter to quickly locate the vehicle, so I faxed the description around the area and drove around the parking lots of dealers looking for the car. I had no luck. A week went by, then two weeks. My mother-in-law was letting us use her Plymouth Duster which was too small to carry all of us without a good deal of discomfort. Our family of six children simply didn't fit in a two door sedan.

I decided that I should look further away, as far as Washington, DC. I could probably buy a car there off a lot that had served the politicians who would be trading in cars for newer ones. I found no car and returned home very disappointed. Once again I looked diligently in Danville, VA. Finally, I heard of one car of interest.

The salesman said, "I have exactly what you are looking for, but it is not on this lot at the moment. If you wait about 45 minutes, I'll have the car here and show it to you."

In 45 minutes, I saw the car, but I learned that it had been at another dealer's lot. They had a contractual relationship between them that allowed them to sell each other's vehicles. The car was what I wanted, but the price was $4400. I told him that was a problem because I had made a decision to spend no more than $4000. He said he could come down to $4100 and no lower. We stood there and couldn't come to an agreement. I would have been unfaithful to the word of the Lord if I had given in to $4100. I had received that the amount should be no more than $4000. I had made it a principle to receive from the Lord the amount to spend, and I wouldn't spend any more than that. I drove my mother-in-law's car home.

He Inclined His Ear

Another week went by, and we were still having difficulty getting from place to place with my large family. Some of the older children were getting "vocal" about having to ride on top of each other. One morning, my mother-in-law and I went to town to do some shopping in a rather routine manner, but as we were driving down Riverside Drive in Danville, Virginia, I sensed a strong urgency from the Lord to go to a particular car dealer on North Main Street. It required me to turn around and to drive out of my way to get to the car lot. It was a small lot, and I had never had any dealings with this man before. When we arrived, there was a car in the lot that appeared to be exactly what I was looking for. We pulled in and I looked the car over. It was a nine passenger station wagon with low mileage in good working condition.

He had originally asked $4400 for this car, but he had come down to $4000 which was the top figure I had received in faith from God. I was ready to sign the paperwork and finally get our car.

In the course of doing the paperwork, I needed the license plate number from the vehicle that had been stolen to transfer it over. I called my wife and said, "Honey, I have found the car we are supposed to buy! It's just the car we have been looking for and at the right price, but I need the license plate number from our old car."

She said, "You can't buy that car!"

I said, "What do you mean I can't buy that car? I have been praying and seeking God and this is it. I am going to buy the car."

In the back of my mind I was thinking, besides I'm the husband and you are the wife and this is really a decision for me to make. This was early in our marriage, if you know what I mean.

She said, "You don't understand. Just a few minutes ago, I got a phone call from a car dealer in Danville, Virginia, and he said that he had a car to sell exactly like the one you described for $3500."

I said, "It doesn't seem reasonable."

I had looked all over the Washington DC area, and I had sent out faxes in the community, and now you are telling me that there are two cars in the same community that are the same make, model and year, and one man is asking $4400 and the other is asking $3500!

I said, "Honey, thank you for the information."

I hung up the phone and looked at the car dealer and said, "We have an unusual situation here. It appears to me that this car that I am about to give you $4000 for, very possibly doesn't actually belong to you. As a matter of fact, I just learned of another car like this one in Danville, and the dealer offered to sell me the exact same car that is sitting here on your lot for $500 less than you are offering."

The car salesman began hemming and hawing (cough, cough), "Wait a minute, I am going to have to make a phone call," and he asked me to go out of the room. I went out and he made his phone call, and afterwards he called me back into the room.

He said, "I have been in the automobile business for over 40 years. This is the first time in my experience that this situation has arisen. This is very difficult for me and I don't know what to do about it."

As I had been waiting outside the room, knowing that he was talking to the other car dealer, I developed a plan. I said, "Well, I realize your profit is jeopardized,...what you might have received by selling me this car, but I also realize that I don't want to give you $500 more than the other car dealer was asking. So to make you happy, let's do this; I'll give you $3,750 and split the price between your price and his price."

He said, "Okay, we'll do it." I purchased the car and went home.

Shortly after I arrived home, I had a visit, from a good friend, Gary Gaddy, who had worked for me a few years earlier when I was running a newspaper. (As a matter of fact, he worked for me in a very sacrificial way, working for free for a period of time and working for next to nothing for a period after that.) He had just graduated from school and his finances were stretched. As it worked out, I had paid for the new car in such a way that I ended up with several hundred dollars of cash in my hands. Realizing the blessing I had received from the Lord, I was free to give him $700. Not only did I receive more than had been taken from me, but I had even more left over so that I was able to share it with someone else.

He Inclined His Ear

As I said before, this story will never make a soap opera on TV or be made into a movie by Hollywood. It certainly won't be on the five o'clock news, but I am convinced that God interacts with us in a very personable and wonderful way. God, whose purposes are eternal, clearly reveals His hand to show us His goodness. I pray that having heard this story, your expectations in Him might be increased, and you too can live with the hope and possibility of seeing the goodness of the Lord in the land of the living.

By the way, I forgot to mention that the insurance company located our stolen car several weeks later. It was quite salvageable. The young man had also taken some credit cards to pay for gas and food. He had a great trip to California and back. He was re-incarcerated in the very facility that he had originally left. He was back with all his friends with a real story to tell. The tools that he had stolen from me were replaced by the insurance company. I had a new chain saw, carpenter tools and mechanic tools. On hindsight, it was a rather pleasing affair that warms my heart.

W. Stephen Keel

Chapter 7: Is this it, or is there something else?

Not all of everything that occurs in our lives has what we can call a really clear beginning, but what I am about to share had a very clear beginning. On a particular evening, I was driving to my routine prison ministry meeting in Blanch, North Carolina. I was led to ask the Lord the question, "Is this prison ministry the plan that You had for me before the beginning of time….the work that You ordained that I would do; or is there something else, something perhaps larger than this?"

There was a reason I asked this question. I said to the Lord, "I really need to know," because if this is it, then I want to do this particular work with all my heart and all my soul, but if there is something else, then I don't want to miss it. I want to walk in whatever it is that You have designed and desired for me."

My prayer was answered in a way that I could not have anticipated.

We had a young girl in our home, Angie Filimon, who had come to live with us when she was 12 years old. Nancy and I had traveled to Romania to help with the building of an orphanage in 1992 after the fall of Communism in that country. Angie came to us in a rather remarkable way, but that is yet another story. Eventually she attended a Bible college in Barrington, Rhode Island. At the time of her graduation, I traveled to Rhode Island to celebrate her graduation. It was a three-day event with multiple speakers and activities.

At the beginning of the celebration, a pastor/evangelist from Richmond, Virginia, was honored by the college with an honorary degree. As he stood to receive it, remarks were made about his life, his Gospel work in 22 countries, his raising of nine children, and his growing church in Richmond, Virginia. As I was listening to the accolades applied to him, I became jealous. I said "Lord, why did You give this man these opportunities for ministry and leave me hidden away for 30 years in a prison where no one could appreciate my fine ministry to these young men?"

He Inclined His Ear

As soon as I said that, I heard the voice of the Lord say, "Speak to this man."

Because I was in a state of jealousy, I refused. I said, "No way. I am not going to do it!" The urgency to speak to him remained intense for the entire three days of the graduation celebration.

On the second day of the graduation in the wee hours of the morning, my jealousy had turned to a form of agony. To add to the interest of my agony, my heart began to ache, not in an emotional sense but with real pain in my chest. I thought I was having a heart attack. It was one o'clock in the morning, and I was trying to decide what to do. I said to the Lord, "I am ready to go. If You want to take me now, that is fine. I believe that You have demonstrated through all these years that You can take care of my wife and my children. I am not terribly concerned for them. I know they are going to miss me, BUT I really don't want to go now if I haven't yet done the work that was ordained for me before the beginning of time. So, if You want to take me, fine, but if You want to keep me around to do something else You have planned, that is really what I want to do."

The following day I approached one of the speakers at the graduation and told him about the pain in my heart and he prayed for me. I was reluctant to go to a doctor because I didn't have any medical insurance, and I was so far away from home. I didn't want to call my wife and tell her about the problem because I didn't want her to worry and feel pressured to drive to Rhode Island to get me. I endured the pain. It was an ongoing pain,...very scary, but not too severe.

When the event ended, Angie, some of her friends and I travelled to a restaurant about five miles from the college to wait out the several hours before my airplane was scheduled to depart. We were in a restaurant where you can eat all you desire to eat. There was an endless food bar. We ate for quite a while. Just as we were finishing, the pastor that I had refused to speak to came in with his mother and father and sat down at the table next to us. When I saw him sitting there, I knew that this was a set-up from God to deal with my disobedience about speaking to him. My jealousy came back, and in my heart I said emphatically, "I am not going to talk to this guy!"

W. Stephen Keel

We sat at our respective tables and timed passed. By eaves dropping on his conversation, I learned that he wasn't going to leave for another two hours. I saw that I was going to be locked up by God in this restaurant with this man for a long time.

I stood up to get a glass of ice tea. As I walked back past this gentleman's table, he carelessly moved his hand and dropped his fork. Before it could hit the floor, it landed on my foot. I was quite startled. I reached down and picked up the fork and said to him, "The Lord has been telling me to talk to you for three days, and I have been in a state of disobedience, but it is very obvious to me now that I am supposed to speak to you. So, here I am. My name is Stephen Keel. I'm from Danville, Virginia."

He said, "Oh, Danville, Virginia, I was just there two weeks ago. As I was driving through, I stopped my car and the Lord spoke to me and told me to bring my tent here and have an evangelistic crusade. I know that God told me to come to Danville. Is it possible that you know anyone that would be willing to help with the details in setting up a crusade in Danville?"

At that time, I was part of a prayer meeting of a group of six men who had been meeting together for several years. One of the topics that had come up from time to time was the need for a tent. Dr. Hooker would say about once a month, "We need to get a tent and tell people about Jesus."

I told the fork-dropping preacher that there was a possibility that I knew some people who might help. "I'll take your name and number and call you back when I find out."

The pain continued in my chest as I headed for home. I caught the plane and took my designated seat next to the God-appointed passenger. I have to confess that I am nervous about riding on airplanes next to attractive women. My life before Christ was ruled by what the Bible calls lust and inordinate affection. I know that I am a new creature in Christ and that old things have passed away and that all things are become new. I also know that the devil is like a roaring lion seeking those whom he can devour. The number of men of God who have fallen into the "other woman" trap is significant, so I, in light of my history and knowledge of the ways of the devil, purposefully avoid situations that can be problematic. This particular passenger was not only pretty, she was obviously very intelligent.

I really believe that the Lord has a sense of humor. Arthur Burt has said, "As soon as we fix the fix that God has fixed to fix us, He fixes another fix to fix us." I could not fix this fix. I was going to have to ride next to this attractive woman. Before long, the Lord revealed how He was going to fix this particular fix.

Per chance, that is coincidently, the lady was a cardiologist working as the director of a research program at Johns Hopkins University. Her research targeted heart conditions in men of my age with my medical background. After telling her all about the pain in my chest and my fears generated from my father's medical heart history, she told me that if I would call her, she could arrange for me to become a participant in the research program. As a participant in the program I could receive all of my medical treatments at no cost. This was good news because I did not have any health insurance. Of course I was already benefiting from the program in that she had just taken a complete medical history from me, and I was not paying for an expensive doctor's office visit. It seemed to me that the Lord was fixing multiple fixes simultaneously.

As our conversation progressed, I mentioned to her that I played racquetball as often as twice a day. She said that she too played racquetball. What a coincidence! Just as we were approaching landing she told me that she was confident that I did not need to enroll in the research program. It was her professional opinion that I had strained a muscle in my chest playing racquetball and that I should use a little ice and enjoy the rest of my life.

I returned home and told the men what had happened. They got a laugh out of my meeting the pretty doctor, and then they said the whole thing sounded like God to them. "Let's go ahead and have this tent revival."

We called and made arrangements, planning the tent revival for the city of Danville, Virginia. One of the desires I had for the revival was that it be interracial. One of the ways to accomplish this was by having an interracial music ministry. I had heard a singing group a few months earlier, a black Gospel women's quartet. It seemed that if I could find these people and invite them to sing, it might help us attract people of color to the meeting. I didn't know the name of the group, but I did know about a black radio station in Yanceyville, North Carolina. I assumed the people there would know the people in the singing group. I made a phone call and sure enough, the owner of the station, George Thaxton, knew the group and gave me their phone number.

George said, "So you are having a tent revival. Why don't you come to the radio station and tell us about the tent revival. You can go on the air on Friday morning at 10am when we have a call-in show, and you can tell our audience all about it."

I said, "Okay."

Friday came along and I told the story of the tent revival. At the end of the program, George said that since the revival hadn't occurred yet and since we do this every Friday morning, why didn't I come back next Friday morning and tell them the same story. I could continue to promote the tent revival. I told him I would be glad to do it again. I went in the following Friday morning, and he asked me to come back a third time.

The revival occurred. Then the manager said, "The people are enjoying your being here on Friday mornings. Why don't you come and do this on a regular basis?"

I said, "Okay. That sounds good to me."

I became part of a radio program where the assistant manager, Leroy Conley and I received phone calls and talked about things in the Bible. This went on for about two months. One particular Friday morning, it changed. I was sitting in one control booth and the Leroy was sitting in the other control booth. We both had access to the telephone. I listened to him talking to the radio audience.

He said, "Today is the last day that Brother Steve is going to help me with the radio program."

Then there was a long pause. I thought, "Well, I have been kicked out before, but I don't think I have ever been so publically dismissed! This is interesting."

He Inclined His Ear

Then he said, "The reason this is the last day that Brother Steve is going to help me, is because next week this is going to be Brother Steve's program, and if he needs any help from me, which I don't think he will, I will be glad to help him,... but next week this program belongs to Stephen Keel."

That was the beginning of a radio ministry that reaches into the world today in several languages on hundreds of stations. It started when I refused to hear the voice of God. My rebellion required that a fork would be dropped on my foot to allow me access to God's grace. My rebellion also led to chest pain to get my attention and eventually help me to repent.

I continued to go to the radio station every Friday morning for about a year. The manager of the radio station approached me and said that the people really like to hear me speak, but that at times I am a "little too deep." Sometimes in the course of an hour, the subjects I would get into were too complicated for the audience. I was speaking to an audience that included many with limited knowledge of the Bible. George Thaxton said, "We'd like to ask you to do something. How would you like to come in every morning at 8 a.m. and give us a 15 minute program instead of the hour that you are currently doing?"

I knew there was no way possible I could do that. I had arranged my life to be able to take off Friday mornings and now he was asking for something daily. I told him I didn't think I could do it. I continued for several weeks on Fridays, but I also continued to evaluate his request.

A friend, Jeff Rudd, who was also working in prison ministry, mentioned to me that he was going to do a teaching on the book of Proverbs. When he said that, something stirred within my heart. I considered the fact that for 30 years, I had read a chapter from the book of Proverbs nearly every day. That meant I had read the book of Proverbs 12 times every year. It occurred to me that maybe I had learned something by doing this, and there might be something I could give back from my in-depth study.

I went back to the radio station manager and asked him, "How does this sound to you? I would like to do a verse-by-verse teaching on the book of Proverbs, except I can't come into the station on a daily basis, but I could do it at home. I can make recordings of these programs, and on a weekly basis I can bring them over to you."

He said, "That sounds like a great idea to me."

A Proverb a Day (APAD) was birthed that day. For the next two years, I went to bed at ten o'clock at night, having done research on specific verses. I would wake at 5am and continue to meditate on the Scriptures. Then, I recorded one 14-minute program. At the end of the week, I spent time editing and burning the five programs to CD. It required a considerable amount of discipline to do this. More than once, I was down to the wire getting the CD ready to take to the radio station. Over the next two years I delivered 270 programs. At 8am, Monday through Friday, my wife, my mother-in-law, and I would sit in the living room and listen to the programs on radio.

We would say to ourselves frequently, "That's a pretty good program. A lot of people need to hear that."

George's wife told me that APAD had become her daily bread. It was leading her in her spiritual life. Once I visited a small church in a nearby community and the guest speaker preached the message that I had preached on the air that very week. The speaker, a young woman, had heard the program and been inspired to re-teach it verse for verse and Scripture for Scripture! She didn't mention that she had copied it from my radio program, so you can imagine her surprise when I introduced myself to her after the church service!

These experiences led me to say to the Lord, "It seems to me that this program could use a wider audience than the one that it currently has. Is there some way possible that You could open it up to other radio stations and maybe to other languages and places in the world? We'd enjoy watching You do that."

My wife and I had prayed along those lines for several weeks when a friend of mine, Pastor Ignace Augustin from Haiti, came to visit us. He had a doctor's appointment locally and needed a place to stay. He and his wife, Franchette, often stayed with us when they were in town.

He Inclined His Ear

I gave them copies of the audio CD's of the radio programs and asked, "Brother, would you listen to these and ask yourself the question whether or not these would be of any benefit to the people of Haiti."

Three days later he came to me and said, "Brother Steve, my wife and I have listened, and we believe that this material is for Haiti. I have a person in Haiti who can translate them into the Creole language, and we can put you in contact with the people at a radio station in Haiti."

I received that as an answer to prayer. Within a few weeks, my wife and I were on an airplane travelling to Haiti where we met Lancy Levielle, who became the Creole voice and translator of A Proverb A Day (APAD). We met with the manager of the radio station and made arrangements to pay $10 for every 30 minutes of broadcasting that would reach out to 400,000 people. That amounted to $50 a week, a significant commitment on our part. In addition we needed to pay Lancy and set her up with a computer and recording equipment.

Then the real battle began. Everything that could go wrong went wrong. The computers we were using to do recordings were breaking down. Some people became confused about their role in the project relative to Internet access and office space issues. Lancy was working in 110 degree heat in a small room. It seemed that there was no way that this program would actually materialize, but six months later we began broadcasting A Proverb A Day in the country of Haiti.

Not long after that, I met Michael Escalante who invited me to go to Acapulco to the Christian Radio Broadcasters conference in Mexico. Part of my interest in going was to see if the program could be translated into Spanish and broadcast to the Mexican people. Just like in Haiti, we didn't have a budget. We were not pastors of a large congregation with mission budgets and fund raising systems. I had no significant means to make this come to pass, but I did have a willingness, and I was available.

The conference center on the beach had about 300 people in attendance. I noticed an attractive lady who was obviously by herself. My wife was not with me on this trip, so I made a decision that I would not speak to this lady because it wasn't wise for me to speak to her without my wife. I felt it was inappropriate.

At the end of the conference as everyone was leaving, Michael Escalante came to me and said, "I have a word from the Lord for you. There is a woman at this conference that God has told me that you are supposed to speak to. I left her sitting at a table on the other side of the conference area, and you need to go there right away because she has to leave immediately."

He took me to the table, and there was the very lady that I said that I wouldn't speak to. Within a few minutes, I learned that she was a Christian journalist who had recently gone to Australia to assemble a team of translators to translate newscasts for the World Olympics in the Spanish language for a Christian news press in Mexico and Spain. Because she had a track record of assembling teams of translators, she felt that there was a possibility that she could arrange for APAD to be translated into Spanish.

We only spoke for 20 minutes, but it was enough to kindle a relationship between myself and Magdalena Latorre, who became the general editor and the Spanish voice of "Un Proverbio al Dia". As I am writing these memoirs,[1] APAD is being broadcast in 26 countries on about 300 radio stations.

The goal, the main reason for writing this book and for telling this story, is to make you aware of the fact that you too can hear the voice of God. You can experience some of the marvelous things that can occur when you talk to Jesus and Jesus talks to you. You can expect to see results in a meaningful and powerful way. It happened to me. My interest in hearing the voice of God was inspired by people whom I had met, who told me their powerful stories when they had listened the voice of God.

---

[1] 2008

Chapter 8: Headaches

How the Lord speaks to us and reveals Himself to us in marvelous ways! In the instance of the prolonged headache, I recall having sought the Lord continually. When you have this kind of pain and it is so intense, you can't ignore it. You will try anything for relief: you will take medicine; you will take showers; you will jog; you will relax; and you will do everything you can to deal with the pain.

After several days of a certain spectacular headache, I had done all of these things. The Lord arranged events so that I was on the lawn on a summer evening with my wife and another young couple who had recently come to the Lord. We were talking about the things of God, about the process of receiving grace from the Lord Jesus Christ.

I discovered that the young man was living an unfulfilled life as a professing Christian. He had been to a church service and felt the conviction of the Holy Spirit. He had gone to an altar in response to an invitation. When he left the altar, some people told him that he had become a Christian and he was saved. He did not perceive any reality related to his salvation experience. He had been told that he was saved, but he couldn't prove it to himself in any way. He was only attending church regularly because it was expected of him as a "new Christian."

When he told me this, I was able to talk to him about the difference between "accepting" Jesus and "receiving" Jesus. As it happens, there is a broad misconception in the body of Christ that states that one need only "accept Jesus." I explained to him that the difference between accepting and receiving has a lot to do with whether God was controlling the event or whether he was.

If one accepts the Lord, that implies that somehow, salvation is in one's own power; he can adjudicate or authenticate and tell himself that he has decided that Jesus is the Son of God. In some manner the one who accepts the truth validates the veracity of the truth in his life by his acceptance of it. I pointed out to him that that process of acceptance was a rather willful and self-centered activity. What was really implied in the Scripture was this, "As many as RECEIVED him, to them He gave power to become the Sons of God."

I used an illustration of a glass having water poured into it. Prior to the pouring, it was empty, but once it received the water, it was full. Jesus told us that we could be filled with the Holy Spirit. We don't fill ourselves. We receive it.

As I explained this to him, we took a moment and prayed and asked the Lord to give him grace to "receive" life in Christ, that the very energy of the Holy Spirit would be poured into the tabernacle of his body, that he would be renewed and come alive in Christ. As we were pursuing this I was still experiencing the headache. I realized that I needed to "receive" the healing the same way that he was receiving life in Christ, so I lay on my back, and I looked up at the stars beholding the handiwork of God. I relaxed and "received" the healing I had sought with my volition for so many days! The pain in my head evaporated. I sat up, and I was totally and completely healed.

This is not intended to be an exhaustive treatise on how to deal with headaches. I am mentioning this merely to say that God is the God of the headache, and I have personal experience where there is no question in my mind that my interaction with the Lord Jesus Christ in the realm of the Spirit was clearly and specifically the process by which I was delivered from these very severe migraine headaches.

Having experienced that, I have faith to pray for other people with headaches. That doesn't mean that every time I pray for people, they get delivered. Many times pain is there for a purpose. The Lord has enabled us to have receptors of pain because He wants to teach us something. He wants to show us something. Until we are fully engaged in His purpose, we can not necessarily expect the healing we are seeking.

Many years later I was engaged in prison ministry, which I mentioned earlier. The young men were in maximum custody. I couldn't hold a religious meeting in a room or counsel an inmate privately. My only recourse was to enter the cell block area and sit in the long hallway with 12 cells on one side and 12 cells on the other side. All I could see were steel doors with openings where the food trays were passed through at meal times. There were also 12 x 12 inch squares with

He Inclined His Ear

metal doors that could be opened or shut by the prisoner allowing someone to talk to them.

My normal practice was to enter and to greet each man individually before I actually began the ministry of the Word. One particular day as I got to the tenth cell on the right-hand side, I looked in and saw a young man who was having a severe migraine headache. I was very familiar with the symptoms. I'd "been there and done that."

I looked at him and said, "It's clear to me that you have got a really bad headache. How would you like to have me pray for you so that the Lord could deliver you from this pain?"

He looked at me and said, "I'm a Muslim."

I said, "Well, I don't see that as a problem. You have flesh and blood, and God sent his Son into the world that the world might be saved. That qualifies you as a recipient of my prayers. Do you mind if I pray?"

He said, "No, I don't mind."

So, I prayed and simply asked that the Holy Spirit would invade this cell with His presence and that the healing virtue of Christ would remove the pain from this young man's head and that he would be healed in the name of Jesus.

After I prayed, at the prompting of the Spirit, I said to him, "I know you are still having the headache, but I am going to be in this cell block for about an hour and a half, ministering the Word and singing. I am confident that when I come back to visit you afterwards, you are going to be totally and completely delivered from this headache. Enjoy the health you are about to experience and God bless you."

I continued my tour of the cell block greeting the men and followed up with the pattern of singing and preaching that God had given me. When I finished, I went back to his cell block and looked in. Just as I had previously seen clearly that the man had a headache, I now saw clearly that the man had been delivered from it. I said to him, "Well, I see your headache is gone."

He said to me, "Yes. And my Momma is a Baptist."

He then said, "I have had this headache for four days continuously and now it is gone."

Alleluia, that is possible in Christ. That instantaneous deliverance occurs in conjunction with the hearing of the voice of God. In closing this small section on headaches, I would like to point out, that what you just read does not involve some evangelist that has been promoted over the air waves via television or satellite calling people into a room with a lot of anticipation and eagerness, nor does it involve healing lines with intense music and the building up of faith through testimonies. Everything that you have heard involves a man who is rather unknown by the world, but is known by God, a man to whom God inclined His ear. If He inclined His ear unto me, He will incline His ear unto you also. Amen.

More Healings

I have already discussed how hearing the voice of God enabled me to be free from headaches. Our corporate relationship with Christ relative to healings has been both a blessing and problematic within the body of Christ.

I believe the problem has been aggravated as charlatans have used the power of God to heal as a fund-raising device. I know that the world has taken great joy in exposing these charlatans. Every time they have had the opportunity to expose hypocrisy in some prominent Christian, it has been been used to justify aversion to Christianity. The Lord shows clearly that the reason people don't come to the light is that they loved the darkness more than they loved the light. That is easily translated into saying, "I want nothing to do with Jesus, because if I do, I will have to stop doing the sinful things I like. I don't want to stop, so I am not going to come to the light."

In spite of the fact that the body of Christ has always been abused by charlatans, the fact still remains that "He sent His Word and He healed them."

Jesus still touches those with infirmities and the infirmities evaporate. Today many people continue to obtain the benefits of the love of God as they reach out to the Savior for healing. I have received many,

many healings. I have already told you about the headaches that disintegrated under the power of God.

On another occasion, I had a serious bout with gout. (Is this good poetry, "A bout with the gout"?) It stayed with me for months.

This led me to study gout only to learn that the medical world has one answer for it: continuous medication for the rest of my life. Scholars described this as a condition that can't be healed. I hoped that it could be healed for me. I had seasons of pain that were so severe that I was sure I couldn't stand it any longer. One night, I found myself standing in a Christian meeting engaged in a conversation with a precious sister in the Lord who had recently been healed of cancer. Having been healed, she had faith. She said, "Let me pray for you." When she prayed for me, instantly the pain in my big toe went away, and twenty years later, it is still gone. I have had no recurring episodes of gout.

In this instance, someone prayed for someone else who needed healing. The Scripture teaches us that we can comfort others the comfort we have been comforted with. Now that I am healed, I have had numerous opportunities to pray for others to be healed.

Now let me tell you how God answered my wife when she was desperate to know His will for her life. My wife had pursued a career of beauty and desire for fame. She had been a beauty pageant winner in her younger years. She pursued the dramatic arts and singing, hoping to become well-known. Instead of becoming well-known, she became a Christian. As a Christian, the stage life she had pursued was not what Christ had in mind for her as a believer. She had to set aside those aspirations of her life, and the prominence that she had wanted in the world. She still wanted prominence, but she wanted it now in Christ.

She was still attracted to the stage life. She looked at people like Kathryn Kuhlman, who had a wonderful relationship with God that allowed her to speak healing into many people's lives. Kathryn was greatly used of God and had international prestige and fame as an evangelist. She ministered from city to city in large auditoriums with tens of thousands attending to receive healing from God. Nancy expected and looked for a ministry similar to Kathryn's. She clung to this desire for about a year. Soon she entered into a deep prayer-life about it. When no encouraging answers were forthcoming, she changed her prayers and aspirations to be satisfied with any kind of prominence with God, even if it was not the stage.

Finally she was led to ask God a question point blank. "What is the highest call of a woman?" She believed this was the correct way to pose the question. She didn't want to ask for the highest call of a "person" but made it gender specific. She didn't hear any answer for the next year. Actually she didn't *want* to hear the answer that God had. It took that long for her to get prepared to hear it. Finally she heard in the smallest voice, an almost crazy idea that couldn't be God! The only reason she entertained it at all was that it was the LAST thing she would think up on her own, and absolutely the last thing in the world she wanted to do. The still small voice said, "The highest calling of a woman is to be a mother."

Nancy already had two children. She had had them reluctantly because she didn't want to lose her figure or be tied down to raising them. She thought that somehow it would erode her beauty. Little did she know that having children would turn her into a very beautiful mature Christian woman. After she received an answer to her question, she needed to respond to God. She was glad she hadn't heard the calling earlier because she wasn't ready to bow her knee to this answer, but now she was ready to do whatever God thought best.

She replied to God at the same moment He spoke to her: "God, if this is You talking to me, give me twins as a sign." She added a second request: "Please send me a hand-maiden to help me." She sought to do wholeheartedly whatever God wanted. He heard her reply and in a matter of several months she was expecting twins. She had a good pregnancy and carried them to full term. When she went into labor, I went with her into the delivery room. She used the Lamaze Method or Husband Coached Method for labor, so that she did not take any medication during labor.

The first twin was born without incident, Marguerite Marie, but the second twin, Melissa Mae had a problem. The problem was a prolapsed cord, meaning the umbilical cord presented first, and the baby was pressing against it so that she was not getting any oxygen. Melis-

He Inclined His Ear

sa was in breach position, not uncommon for second twins, which meant she could not be born without medical intervention. The doctor was aware of the situation because the fetal heart monitor went silent.

The doctor said, "I have two minutes to save the baby."

There wasn't time for a Caesarean section. That would involve moving my wife to a different floor in the hospital for general surgery and going under general anesthesia. This doctor had served in Vietnam where he had a lot of experience with deliveries of Vietnamese babies with almost non-existent medical facilities. He decided to physically remove the baby. He reached inside the womb and grabbed the child by one foot. He could not get his hand on the second foot before time ran out. He was forced to pull the second child out by one foot. She weighed 5 lb. 5 oz. This was an extremely painful experience and a very dangerous one. The doctor said later that Nancy should have been put to sleep for that procedure.

But, grace being grace, as my wife was experiencing the pain, we began worshipping the Lord. We sang as the baby was born, "What shall take away my sin? Nothing but the blood of Jesus."

Immediately after the baby was born, we saw that she was totally blue and lifeless. She did not breathe. Facing the visible evidence of disaster, I found myself on my knees with my hands raised in the air singing, "This is the day that the Lord has made. We will rejoice and be glad in it."

The room was filled with commotion. A couple of nurses and the doctor were working frantically on Melissa while we were singing. There was a little question regarding our sanity, but intense things happen in intense situations.

As we sang the phrase, "We will rejoice and be glad….," I heard a cry. It was the cry of the baby who had been revived and given back life. It was Melissa. She lived. By the next day we had the final medical results that she was healthy with no brain damage.

While he was telling me that the child was healthy outside the delivery room, I was in a state of true anguish. I experienced an intense sense of unbelief. Even though I had seen a miracle, and even though the doctor had come to me and told me I had just seen a miracle, I struggled with fear of not being able to provide for this burgeoning family. I was broken and humbled thinking I couldn't possibly do it. As an antidote to my unbelief, I heard the Lord say, "As I have given you this family, I will also provide for the future of your family."

That was 30 years ago, and it has been fulfilled. We have raised seven children of our own and another one from Romania; they have been cared for, brought through college, and are living successful lives. Incidentally, the handmaiden was my mother-in-law who moved in after the twin's birth to help Nancy, and she has lived with us ever since, cooking, gardening and helping take care of the children.

An experience of this intensity has multiple ramifications.

In spite of the blue lifelessness of the baby, we had grace to exercise and act on the revelation that praise is the right response in extreme circumstances. It was the sacrifice of praise. We prayed and sang, "This is the day that the Lord hath made. We WILL rejoice and be glad in it." Then when Melissa breathed, we were exceedingly glad.

When Melissa was two and a half years old, she was playing in the parking lot at our home. I did not know she was behind our car, when I started the car and backed it up. The car tire rolled directly over her. (A few years before this happened, Nancy's first cousin's husband had killed one of their children by backing over him with their car.) I heard the "clunk" as my bumper hit her, but I didn't know what it was until I had backed entirely over her body.

I got out of the car and found her lying limp on the gravel with her eyes closed in front of the car bumper. Nancy appeared almost immediately. I picked up the child, and carried her into the living room. We prayed, "Father, in the name of Jesus, redeem this situation! Give Melissa back her life. We can do nothing. You must do everything." Within moments, her eyes opened, so we knew she was alive. Then she moved her hand. The next act required great faith. I lowered her to the floor. She put her feet down and walked away! We could hardly believe it. Her body was not hurt at all! The Lord was available to meet us in our darkest moments.

He Inclined His Ear

Whether or not she was healed of some awful injury is not nearly as miraculous as was our ability to have cool heads and satisfied minds that freed us and enabled us to call on the name of the Lord with our petitions from a state of peace in the midst of a horrific accident.

W. Stephen Keel

Chapter 9: A Miracle among the Maggots

The Lord led me to be a worker in a food distribution program. Twice a week at night, we carried food to three specific families that lived in deep poverty. One of the families lived about five miles away from us. It was a black family with nine small children. Every time I carried food, I read a chapter from the Scriptures. I had gone only twice when the husband of the household, who had been drunk each time I visited, discovered that I was on a regular schedule. After that, he made himself absent when I visited so he wouldn't have to hear the Scriptures. I am not sure why he was so bothered by the reading because he appeared to be passed out on bed when I saw him.

Their poverty was pronounced. The ceiling was so thick with flies that it was barely visible. Dirty diapers lay in the corner of the room with maggots growing in them. Trash filled the yard outside their log home which was located deep in the woods. It was a very difficult situation.

The lady of the house could barely communicate with me. When I asked her what sort of food she needed, her only responses were, "Uhhh" and "Uhhhh, huhhh."

That was it, almost two words! Grace prevailed and over a period of weeks, I continued to bring them food. It became my habit to take one or more of my children with me. We went into the kitchen and put cans of things on the shelves. I am certain that we were being very helpful to that family during that time. They had so little.

We had prayed and read the Scripture in this home for several months when one particular night the father made a huge mistake. He forgot that I was coming. Instead of being absent as he had been before, he was present when I arrived. Thankfully, he was not inebriated this time. I began to talk to him. I asked him, "How did you get into this situation? Why is it that you are not working?"

He said, "I'd like to work, but the only work that I can do is physical labor. I worked in a fertilizer factory. I used to pick up hundred-pound sacks of fertilizer and move them, but two years ago, I was

He Inclined His Ear

shot in my arm. Now my arm is useless. I can't lift anything anymore."

Hearing the voice of God, I simply said to him, "The Lord has given you this family, and He has given you responsibility to care for this family. He loves you very much and He wants you to be able to work. I would like to pray and ask the Lord to restore your arm and make it possible for you to work again."

He didn't object. I laid hands on him and said, "Father, in the name of Jesus, You love this man and his family. This man needs his arm to supply for the needs of his family. I ask You in the name of Jesus to heal this arm, Amen."

We left.

A week later, we came back. As I approached the house, I knew that something had changed. The first indication was that all of the trash in the yard was gone. Firewood was stacked in neat piles on the porch. When we got inside, the flies were gone and the room was in order. I learned that right after I had prayed, this man was healed and the next day he was offered a job. He had returned to work and cash was coming into the house. He wasn't there at that moment, but his wife was. She talked to me for the very first time telling me what had happened. Then I said to her, "How are you doing?"

She said that she was having stomach pain and had had it for a long time. The fact that she was talking and describing her ailment was a miracle because previously she had only said "Uhhhh," to me.

She said she couldn't do anything about her illness, even though Social Services offered her medical attention. She said she could not get a ride to the doctor's office. I said, "Well, if God loved your husband enough to heal his arm, He also loves you enough to heal your stomach. Let's pray," and we prayed in the name of Jesus, and He healed her. We had an ongoing relationship with this family for some months afterwards allowing us to see the ongoing fruit of the healings. We took them to church with us and had them in our home for a meal. Over time and the great cultural gulf between us, we eventually lost contact with this family.

W. Stephen Keel

Isn't this how the body of Christ is supposed to function? ...each of us responding to God as He leads by His Spirit? This was simply a man with children visiting neighbors who needed help. He had been healed himself so he was able in Jesus name to impart healing to others.

I also think it is profitable to mention that my children observed the Lord's work in this situation carefully. These same children today are serving the Lord. They are not spiritually insensitive. I am confident that there is a relationship between what they saw and who they are.

Oh, go on... (An Expression of Polite Disbelief)

I have tried to avoid telling stories that seemed too outrageous about how God inclined His ear unto me. I think when people try to press a point, they tell stories that border on the outside edge of the possible or the probable. Well, as much as I have tried to avoid the "outrageous", the following is one of those "brink of lunacy" stories.

Dancing with finances as an entrepreneur inevitably creates monetary crisis. When in trouble, ask for help. I had just finished a racquetball game with a brother in the Lord whom the Lord had blessed financially with several thriving businesses.

As we sat naked in the steam room, I shared my dilemma. The brother suddenly stood up and spoke in a very intense voice, "I command the major corporations of the United States of America to purchase computer equipment from Stephen Keel, in the name of Jesus, Amen."

I didn't expect him to say something so wild. Major corporations didn't have any reason to buy computers from me. My customers were supplied by NCR (National Cash Register). I sold almost exclusively to the small business owner. NCR had national account mangers assigned to all of their large corporate accounts, and I was not "in the loop."

I was living in the back waters of Danville, Virginia, a slow city with a dying textile industry. The command struck me as being totally outside of the realm of possibility. Even so, I heard the still small voice say, "Behold, I am the Lord, the God of all flesh. Is there anything too hard for Me?"

He Inclined His Ear

The God of the miraculous is also the God of the unexpected. I went back to my office and received a phone call within the week from IBM Corporation. They wanted to purchase a $150,000 NCR computer. I was a NCR computer reseller. Quite understandably, NCR didn't have anyone in their national organization that was designated as an assigned account manager for IBM. Obviously, IBM made their own computers.

IBM's research and development division was working on a large military project. They found themselves forced by contractual requirements to install computers from multiple vendors in a project being created to run PX's around the world. One of the items they needed was a NCR computer. They called the Buffalo NCR sales office and asked the NCR guy where he could buy a NCR computer. Because of a recent mailing I had done, the NCR guy had in his hand a card with my name on it. He gave my number to IBM and they called me. I sold a $150,000 computer to a major corporation in the United States of America. Subsequently, I found myself supplying file servers and networking equipment to major financial institutions such as Mellon Bank.

I realize that this sequence of events could be attributed entirely to coincidence. I also realize that the steamy brother was not calling on the gods of serendipity. He believed the Scripture that said that what he bound on earth would be bound in heaven. Using his perceived authority as a believer, he issued a command that was fulfilled. I do not advocate making such commands flippantly, but IF Jesus is Lord and if you are in the chain of authority established by His Lordship, you may be called upon to speak outrageously and authoritatively.

Peter and John went to the temple to pray. They met a lame man on the way. Fixing their eyes on him they outrageously said, "Silver and gold have I none, in the name of Jesus Christ of Nazareth, rise up and walk." Now either that was a fairy tale or it actually happened. Because I have been lame and been healed, I believe it actually happened.

In my first year as a believer, Nancy and I moved to the Shenandoah Valley in Virginia to volunteer at a Christian retreat center. Not long after we arrived, I was helping on a construction project. Another

W. Stephen Keel

young man and I discussed issues of faith. I confidently declared that if I were to step on a rusty nail, I would not go to the doctor for a tetanus shot. I would believe God for healing. This position was punctu-punctuated by my observation that rusty nails can cause lockjaw and that lockjaw seemed a frightening way to die.

Within 30 minutes of professing my determination to trust the Lord, I stepped on a nail that was protruding upward through a board on the ground. I felt the rush of pain and simultaneously saw the point of the large nail push upward against the top of my shoe. There is pain and there is exquisite pain. Bathed in the latter, I collapsed on the ground and immediately began crying out to the Lord for healing.

That afternoon, I had an appointment to shoe a horse in a nearby community. I hobbled to the assignment grimacing all the way. At the point where I had one shoe installed on the front of the horse, I nearly fainted. I told the owner that it was impossible for me to finish, in spite of the fact that I would be endangering the horse by leaving the weight of the horseshoe on one foot. I returned home and immediately went to bed. My theological position which I carved out earlier in the day prevented me from even thinking about going to a doctor. I was too exhausted and full of pain to come close to resting. While dancing close to deliria, I began meditating on the purposes of God. Not too long before this I had read "From Prison to Praise," a popular Christian book. Merlin Carothers had recorded how praise had released miracles in his life.

My good friend Arthur Burt has often declared, "First comes the revelation, then, comes the situation to test the revelation."

As I lay in bed suffering, I had a revelation that praise in the midst of pain was a high form of faith. Praise is a statement of confidence in the character of God. Praise embraces God as the controlling Factor, even when bad things happen. Simultaneously, I realized that complaining about pain was the same as spitting in the face of God. Complaining declares that the Lord is weak and helpless, unable to protect and provide appropriately.

Many understand these principles, but at that moment for me, this was deep insight. As I luxuriated in the wonder of these thoughts I had a singular experience. It was as if someone had place a faucet in my

He Inclined His Ear

foot and opened the valve. Literally all of the pain and weariness in my body drained out through the faucet in a matter of seconds. I jumped out of bed and rushed into the next room to tell Nancy the wonderful news of what I had learned and what had happened to me.

The next day, I walked down the steps in the barn to the location where I had left my horse shoeing equipment. The owner was waiting for me. My steps on the stair treads where strong and unfettered. I immediately began telling the story of my zealous declaration of faith, my insight into the value of praise, and my joy at being so dramatically healed.

I Am Worth More Dead than Alive, Not...

In Proverbs it says, "The prudent man sees difficulty ahead and makes preparation for it." I thought my obedience in moving from Roswell, New Mexico back to Virginia was preparing the way to avoid difficulty ahead. Our finances were small but adequate. We had enough money to travel back to Virginia and set up our household in our old home. What I didn't know was that when I returned, I would enter into a period of joblessness. I would find myself in a situation where I would not be able to supply for the needs of my family. I was going to enter into a period of trial and difficulty that was very intense.

When a man is unable to care for his wife and family, it has a profound effect on his pride. His self-image or concept of himself is drastically affected, as was mine during this period of time. I can recall being so discouraged that I felt like I was worth more dead than I was alive. I had a life insurance policy, and I had a constant fantasy of killing myself in such a way that no one would know that it was suicide. Then my wife would be able to collect on the insurance policy and there would be money available to take care of my children. I had many scenarios; some of them involved an automobile accident. I also thought about disappearing. When an attitude of self-destruction comes upon a man, it can grip him tenaciously.

Fortunately I was given a small booklet by Brother Arthur Burt from England. It said that the key to life was surrender. It described totally and completely a surrendered life to the will of God. By grace, that book brought me to a place of surrender, but it was not easy to get there. The last battle occurred on a particular fall afternoon. I had spent hours spinning my wheels doing things that were costing me money instead of making money. I told the Lord, "I would prefer spending my time hearing Your voice, walking in Your Spirit and telling people about Jesus. I commit myself to put my hand to the plow. I will make the business of the kingdom of God first in my life. Please honor and receive me as Your full-time employee."

The commitment was wonderful, but I still had my bias against seminary and being a professional clergyman. I wasn't going to take a religion course. I simply began my new job as a worker in the kingdom of God. I began my work by going to the mall walking around saying, "Okay, Lord, is there anyone here You would like me to talk to? I want to talk only to the people that You want me to."

I spent several days there, and He didn't give me anyone to talk to.

I recall being a bit perplexed. Some brothers in the Lord and I were already having services on Sunday mornings in the local jail. On one Wednesday, I received a call from the captain in charge of the jail. He informed me that our permission to have services in the jail had been revoked. I asked why? He said, "We have a new chaplain and he has brought charges against you, so we have no recourse but to revoke your privileges."

I looked into it further and discovered what had occurred. Good News Prison ministry had hired a full-time chaplain for all of the facilities in the area. Our one service on Sunday mornings wasn't under their auspices or control, and they felt that it should be, but rather than approach me and ask me to join their organization, they chose to remove me from my ministry there.

They justified it on a pretext. We had a new volunteer who wasn't familiar with prison protocol. We typically preached the Gospel on Sunday morning, leading people to Jesus and then counseling with them on Monday night. On the new volunteer's first Monday night, it happened that none of the other volunteers were available to go for the counseling session. He went to the jail and asked the officers to bring the men into the room for a church service. This request was denied because it wasn't part of the policy or practice we had pursued.

He Inclined His Ear

When the new chaplain learned of the "violation of policy and procedures," he requested that our ministry be removed from the list of approved ministries. The captain, endeavoring to please the new chaplain, agreed and did exactly that. We were out!

Not only was I out of the ministry, but that ministry had been my Sunday morning church. I didn't have a job, and I didn't have a ministry either! That resulted in further surrender and brokenness. Ten days later, a man in the community I had never met called me on the phone and told me about a nearby prison that needed a chaplain. An older brother had been working there on a part-time basis, but had to quit due to bad health. I was asked if I would be interested in becoming the chaplain of Blanch Prison.

At that moment, I was not interested at all. In fact, I was rather angry at God for taking away my employment, my church and my ministry, all at the same time. Not wanting to be obstinate, I agreed to meet. We had lunch together. The following day he took me to the prison. He introduced me to the superintendent of the prison who said, "Why don't you take a tour of the facility."

When we walked onto the cell block. the first thing I experienced was extreme fear. I knew that I was walking into a dark and violent environment. The fear remained until I stood in front of one of the cells looking through a 12 inch square hole and began talking to a young man. He told me of some troubling dreams he had had. By the Spirit of the Lord, I began to minister to him. As I ministered to him, the presence of God visited me in a remarkable way. The fear that had wrapped about me was totally dissolved. I knew in my heart of hearts that this was what I was supposed to do.

I finished the conversation and went back to the superintendent's office. I said, "I will do the work."

He said, "The key to the chaplain's office is hanging on the board behind the desk in the sergeant's office. Welcome aboard!"

How remarkable! Blanch Prison was a maximum custody, highly secure prison environment. I didn't even fill out a form with my name and address on it. I was received as a full–time volunteer chaplain with no investigation into my background other than, "Welcome aboard!"

Thus began a four-year encounter with the opportunity to truly serve the Lord with my hand on the plow without looking back. I realize that I may be providing too much detail for many readers. This isn't a story of high drama. It is the story of God enlisting a man into the ministry outside of the ecclesiastical system. It is a story that has been repeated of many men, but is seldom told. I am telling it now to be an encouragement to those who also have been called, and I am telling it to let you know that you may be called also to walk in the power of the Spirit of God without becoming part of the ecclesiastical system.

The prison ministry section of my memoirs is going to be truncated on purpose. In fact, it may have been the most intense period of my life in which I was walking very closely to the Lord. I saw several hundred men receive the Lord, and I became the first chaplain in the institution to baptize inside of the prison. Many experiences were of a profound spiritual nature, and only someone who was there at the time, seeing the powerful battle against evil, would be able to understand what actually happened. Rather than attempt to share those precious experiences, I want to jump ahead to the time when it was over.

After four and one half years of ministry and living like the children of Israel in the wilderness on a day-to-day basis, the superintendent approached me and said that my ministry was appreciated. As the result of the work I had been doing, they realized that they needed a full time chaplain in the facility. They had arranged funding. If I would apply, they would hire me as the full-time chaplain in that institution. I thanked them for the offer, and I considered it before the Lord. I knew that accepting the offer would make me into that which I had determined that I would not become. I would effectively be joining the ecclesiastical system.

I knew from my years working as a volunteer chaplain, that much of the work of an institutional chaplain was somewhat menial in filling out forms, in attending conferences, etc. The application for the position indicated that I needed a degree from seminary with two years of

He Inclined His Ear

clinical training. I didn't have the requisite training requirements. The superintendent responded by saying, "We were aware of that when we gave you the application, but we have seen the value of your ministry in this facility, and we are going to waive the requirements and hire you in spite of the fact that you don't have the qualifications."

That was a very gracious offer on their part; I responded by saying, "The men here know that I am here as a volunteer. My relationship with them would change dramatically if I were to take the job you are offering me. I cannot submit the application."

Two months later, because they had created a budget, they hired a full-time chaplain. It wasn't reasonable for me to continue with a full-time chaplain present, so I graciously left Blanch Prison. Within a week, the same man who had arranged for me to become the chaplain at Blanch, told me that there was an evening ministry available at another facility. He wanted to know if I would take over teaching the Bible there on Tuesday nights. I agreed and spent the next twelve years at Yanceyville Correctional Center.

After the ministry at Blanch Prison ended, I asked the Lord to give me a job. I asked him to give me something I could do that would allow me to provide for the needs of my family. My oldest child Rose of Sharon was preparing to go to college. I knew I needed an income to assist her in her education. Within a month, I found a job working as the marketing director of a software company in Danville, Virginia. It was quite remarkable. In my new position, I had access to the file folder filled with all of the applications of the people who had applied for the job. I discovered I had been given the job over twenty-some applicants, several who had better qualifications than I. They had masters and business degrees and valuable experience.

What I didn't know was that the owner of the company had seen me as a self-starter. He had seen me as an individual who didn't require direction from others. In fact, he had a plan that was consummated within two years. I ended up buying the business from him. That was remarkable because the purchase occurred when I didn't have any money.

I had attended a conference held by Larry Burkett, titled "Business by the Book." Almost immediately I needed the counsel it taught me.

W. Stephen Keel

One of the principles he promoted was that a transaction could be entered into either with "your price and my terms" or "my price and your terms." Though the owner of the company had a high price on the business, my terms were that it would be paid for out of profits over years to come if there were no dramatic changes. In other words, I owed payments as long as I was able to make money in the business I had purchased from them.

I went from having a seven thousand dollar a year income to managing a business with three and a half million dollars in sales in four years. How does something like this happen? How does Joseph who was in prison, one day get a signet ring with power over all Egypt? God has a way of working with men! He put me into this multi-million dollar business environment. I had followed His leading in the details of the purchase, and He prospered the business.

It is not important to give you the details of the computer business other than to say, I developed a national business that sold computers into banks, hospitals, and industry. I didn't know at the time that knowledge of information technology would be an important part of my future ministry.

I had entered into a contract with NCR to do national sales for all of their maintenance people in the country. The week after I signed the contract, an announcement was made: "NCR, having been in business for 104 years will no longer exist. It has been purchased by AT&T."

I had heard rumors of this, but there was no certainty that it was really going to happen. The $50,000 I had invested in positioning myself for the national contract was lost overnight. "The Lord giveth; the Lord taketh away."

Proverbs says that the prudent man sees trouble coming, and he prepares for it. I had made an application to become an authorized AT&T reseller. Because AT&T purchased the assets of NCR, many of the employees from NCR, with whom I had been working, were now AT&T employees. The original obligation to pay a large amount of money for the purchase of the computer business evaporated overnight. My contract with the original owner stated clearly that I would continue to pay him royalties as long as I was a NCR reseller. When NCR was sold to AT&T, NCR ceased to exist, so it was no longer

He Inclined His Ear

possible to pay royalties on NCR sales. The $50,000 I lost creating the national NCR contract was substantially less than the amount I would have been obligated to pay had I continued to be an NCR reseller.

As an AT&T reseller, I began to work with another group of people. Clearly, the Lord did not intend for me to be a computer reseller forever. He caused AT&T to go through a major structural overhaul. They made a decision, that any reseller who was not achieving $20,000,000 a year in revenues would no longer be eligible to do business with them. They severed their relationship with me. But, the Lord had a plan, and if you continue reading, you will discover how a fight with the computer put me into the chicken coop business.

Chapter 10: Royal Priests

There are four straight-forward, simple, yet very important lessons to be discovered from reading these stories.

1. God speaks to us.
2. He hears us when we speak.
3. He is the divine Choreographer. He is involved in every detail of our lives.
4. We can be used as ministers of the Most High without becoming "paid preachers."

These lessons can be illustrated in a series of events that occurred in 1986. I have already mentioned that prior to moving to New Mexico, we had been part of a church where sin was revealed in the camp. Many members became disillusioned and left the church.

When we returned from New Mexico, it seemed to me that the Lord had given me a commission to act as an agent of reconciliation between disaffected brothers and sisters in Christ. I realized that to do that, I would not be able to align myself to the current membership or to those who had left the church. Some way I would try to function as a bridge between the two groups. If you have ever tried to walk in such a role, you realize that it is almost impossible. You become subjected to criticism from both sides of the controversy. That is exactly what happened.

The pastor of the church, Robbie Lea, was upset regarding my efforts. He felt that I was being destructive rather than constructive. Robbie asked Pastor Paul Gordon from nearby to visit me to point out the error of my ways. When they arrived, we sat on the front porch of my house. Tension filled the air. I knew that Robbie had "called the meeting" because he believed that correction was needed. He was following the biblical pattern to bring it about.

Paul said, "Let me hear your side of the story."

He Inclined His Ear

I took a few moments to explain to him some of the history of things that had happened, and how I had been led of the Lord to act as a minister of reconciliation. To the surprise of Robbie and me, Paul laid hands on me and prayed a blessing. He spoke a word of prophecy, effectively confirming the word of the Lord I had received.

Robbie, who had expected to hear a rebuke, responded in a remarkable way. As he was preparing to leave "the meeting," he turned to me and said, "I am going to Haiti next month for two weeks. Would you consider traveling with me and ministering along side of me?"

I was flabbergasted that he invited me, but I knew this must be the Lord, because he was acting contrary to his own will. He wanted to follow with the Holy Spirit, not his own will.

I said immediately, "Yes, brother. I'll go with you." This was my first trip to a foreign country for the purpose of ministering the Gospel of Jesus Christ.

A focus of these memoirs is to reveal how it is possible for anyone who has been born again to walk in the ministry of reconciliation. Jesus was in God reconciling the world to the Father. We who are new creatures in Christ have been given that ministry too. Observation leads me to believe that many people have abdicated their God directed role by deciding that ministry belongs to those who are paid to do it. In 2 Peter he refers to "priests." We are "royal priests." As such, we should function whether or not we are ordained by men. In truth, we are ordained by God.

The airplane ride from Miami to Haiti began a sequence of interesting events. A young Haitian woman sat next to me on the airplane. I noticed immediately that she was very nervous. I could actually see the spirit of fear that possessed her. After a period of time, I began a casual conversation with her. I was able to ask her why was she was so nervous. She explained that she was a business person in Port-au-Prince and that there were many other Haitians on the airplane. She said it was dangerous for her to be seen sitting next to an American, because it might be construed that her seat arrangement was an indication of some form of partnership she had with me. That partnership could be for political purposes or financial purposes, and if some partnership was perceived, she was endangered. She could be attacked for this later.

When she revealed that fear to me, I showed her in the Bible that there is no fear in the perfect love of God because the love of Jesus takes away all the fear from our hearts. We had a period of ministry and then we arrived in Port-au-Prince.

The first thing I encountered when we left the airport and began driving into the city of Port-au-Prince was a spirit of fear which gripped the city. I saw the desperation on the faces of the people. It occurred to me that in that desperation, there was serious danger. I spent several hours speaking to myself out of the Scriptures to get relief from the fear myself, and eventually I found rest and even relaxation in Christ.

Having had this initial experience with nationwide fear, I took advantage of an afternoon to spend time with a song leader of the church. He spoke a little bit of English and was able to help translate from English into Creole the little song that says, "There is no fear in the perfect love of God because the love of Jesus takes away all the fear from our hearts."

I memorized the Creole words to the song and kept that little song going in my heart during the 11 days I was in Haiti.

An annual Baptist convention was held while we were in Les Cayes. Up to 5000 people attended with many invited guest speakers. Dr. J. L. Williams spoke (he is from North Carolina about 40 minutes from where I live in Virginia). He was the only preacher that spoke English. At the time I heard him speak, I didn't know who he was.

His message was based on the Scriptures where Jesus fed the multitudes. Jesus spoke to His disciples and said, "You feed them."

They said, "Master, it doesn't seem possible."

He asked them, "What do you have?"

They answered, "There is a small boy here with a few fish and loaves of bread."

Jesus said, "Give them to Me."

He Inclined His Ear

He broke the bread and fishes and gave them to the disciples. The food was multiplied until everyone was fed with some left over. Dr. Williams exhorted the listeners to realize that they too could feed the multitudes. All that was required of them was to bring the piece of bread or fish or some small item that they had, and place it in the hands of Jesus. He would multiply it, and it would accomplish the goal that it was intended for.

Toward the end of the conference on Saturday night, I found myself at one o'clock in the morning struggling with the voice of God and the urging of the Holy Spirit. I was receiving from the Lord that I was supposed to introduce the song regarding "fear" to the leadership of the conference and subsequently to all of the conference attendees. I wasn't a member of the association or a friend of anyone that was attending. It struck me as an unreasonable expectation that I might somehow be used to speak to those people.

As I was struggling, I could hear outside of my window, the sounds of a voodoo funeral: screeching, wailing, drumbeating, and people willfully engaging in various forms of demon possession. They ingested the spirits! What came out of their mouths was quite frightening, the sounds of animals, and pitiful moaning of unholy spirits. This continued until daybreak. I thought they would have stop then, but they continued into the next day while I was still struggling with God. At a certain point, I submitted. I said, "Lord, even though it appears totally impossible, I receive that You are speaking to me. I will pursue the matter tomorrow to try to share this song with Haiti."

As soon as I made the decision, a sweet peace settled over me, and I was able to sleep. The next morning, I mentioned to the pastor I was visiting, Pastor Ignace Augustin, that God had spoken to me and told me to introduce this song at that convention.

Pastor Ignace said, "That won't happen. Not only do they have choirs from all over Haiti that are scheduled to sing, but they have multiple pastors speaking, as well. The schedule for this event is written in concrete. Each item is timed to the minute, and they can't veer from it because they have to move from one event to the next event. You simply won't be able to do it."

I said, "Okay, I understand, but I really believe that God has spoken to me."

Having heard the exhortation from him, I went to the site of the conference and pursued what seemed reasonable to me. I thought, "I will find J. L. Williams and tell him about the song, and maybe he will see the value of it. Then when he speaks, he will mention it in whatever he has to say to the congregation." What I didn't know was that J. L. Williams had already gone home. I couldn't find him.

I was standing close to the assembly hall bewildered by the fact that God had spoken without giving me a pathway to follow through. Soon I noticed the pastors leaving together from an adjacent building to go to the conference hall. They came out in a column walking two by two. There were about thirty of them marching along a dirt path. Responding to the urgency of the Lord, I approached the man who was at the head of the line, assuming he was in charge. The entire line stopped!

I didn't speak Creole, and he didn't speak English. All I had were the words of the song on a piece of paper in Creole. I handed them to him and I said, "The Lord has given me this small fish, and I want to place it in his hands so that he can feed the multitudes."

Evidently someone in the line understood some English. He spoke to the leader, and the leader looked at me and pointed for me to get in line behind him. I joined the column of pastors.

We entered the conference center where five thousand people had arrived. I was seated on the platform with the other men. Then the meeting began. The singing was exuberant, and everyone who spoke was given great swelling "Amens!"

I couldn't understand a thing. The audience responded to almost every phrase from each of the speakers. Before long, a brother tapped me on the shoulder and said, "They are introducing you. It's your turn."

Not speaking Creole, I hadn't even noticed I was being introduced, but I took it by faith that I was supposed to stand up.

They gave me the microphone, and I said, "Greetings in the name of the Lord, Jesus Christ."

He Inclined His Ear

As soon as I finished speaking, there was a profound silence. In my heart, I said to myself, I have really blown it. These people simply do not want to receive me. I have hugely missed the voice of God. The next thing I heard was a resounding "Amen!"

What had happened was they hadn't understood what I said in English, and it was only after the interpreter spoke to them in Creole that they were able to respond. Instantly I recognized what had occurred so I went ahead and shared a greeting and the little song in Creole.

Evidently this was a great blessing not only to all the people at the conference but to the entire nation of Haiti. The program was broadcast live over Radio Lumiere to audiences all over the country. Later that day, an English speaking missionary who had heard me on radio, called me up and asked me speak to the missionaries at their Sunday evening meeting. This would be an "English" meeting of about thirty missionaries. Normally one of the missionaries gives a 15-minute homily, and they sing a couple of hymns and go home.

He asked me to share the homily. I entered the meeting thinking, I don't know what I can do in 10 or 15 minutes. I began by speaking out of Jeremiah, about how those who trust in man would be frustrated; about a life lived in futility. Then I mentioned how those who trusted in God would be profitable and fruitful. As I opened the Scripture, I applied it directly to our roles as ministers of the Gospel and discussed the fine line between being a missionary in the flesh and being a missionary in the Spirit. The audience was responding with interactions that allowed me to preach for well-over an hour. I believe that this entire sequence of events was a blessing to the nation of Haiti; reminding them that there is no fear in the perfect love of God.

One of the difficulties of being a minister of the Word of God and not being a member of the ecclesiastical system is that one seldom gets an opportunity to speak to the body of Christ. In fact, most of the ministering I have done in the realm of teaching and preaching have been to people outside the body of Christ. Mine has been essentially an evangelistic ministry. After years of wondering if anyone would ever ask me to speak in church, I largely surrendered and bowed to the reality that it simply wasn't going to happen. Nonetheless, the Lord wanted me to see that His purposes could be fulfilled in spite of my low expectations.

In 1992, my wife and I traveled to Romania. We had met a pastor from Romania at a church meeting in Illinois. He told us he was taking a group of Christians into Romania. This was not long after the revolution and the overthrow of the dictator, Ceausescu and the Communist Party. All and all, the invitation was quite exciting, particularly because I had specifically prayed for the believers in the churches in the Communist-bloc countries in years past. Now I would be able to actually go and visit them.

We had some uncertainties about going. We had dedicated our income tax refund to the purchase of tickets and had made reservations well in advance of the trip. As time got closer to the actual date, it was clear that we didn't have the finances to go on the 21-day trip. We had the additional problem of leaving our business at a time when the cash flow was restricted. Meeting payroll was a problem. I responded to the crisis by declaring to the Lord, that I didn't want to go to Romania unless He wanted me to go, and I needed evidence that He wanted me to go.

The evidence would include the financial provision needed at home while I was away. I said, "Lord, if You don't provide for the trip, then I will cancel the trip even though we have already paid for two tickets that cost of $2000."

I would rather lose the $2000 than go anyway and lose even more money. He heard the request and He inclined His ear. Ten days before we left, the finances for the payroll and the trip came in the form of business activity with enough profit to take care of the needs.

Now, being more assured that the Lord wanted us to go, I found myself on the night before we left, in another dilemma. This was it: I was deeply concerned that since there were 30 people on the trip, including a number of pastors, that I would find myself in a role of carrying the suitcases and effectively sitting in the back pew. My mind and my heart were deeply invested in a desire to share the Words of God that were burning in my heart. I felt I had a purpose in ministering the Gospel in Romania.

He Inclined His Ear

At one o'clock in the morning under the stars, I cried out to the Lord and said, "If I am not going to be used as a minister of the Word of God, I don't want to go. I would rather stay home. I can sit in the back pew of a church right here in my hometown. Why travel that great distance and not be used as a tool in the hand of God? So I ask You, in the name of Jesus, open the door for me to speak."

When we arrived in Austria, one of the first things that happened was no one met us at the airport. My wife and I found ourselves in the airport without the ability to speak to anyone. We didn't know how to use the payphone, let alone how to get transportation to the missionary headquarters. We rested and prayed. I heard Him say that I should look in the phone book to locate the name of the person we were visiting. I managed to exchange money and dialed the payphone with a little help. (Phones in different countries each have their own numbering systems.) The brother on the phone told us to take a taxi and gave us an address. When we arrived, I could tell we were not high priority on the list of guests.

Others had come from many countries, including Germany, Japan, Mexico and Sweden. At the first meal, the leader of the trip addressed us and said, "There are four men who will be speaking in the churches as we move through the country in the next twenty days."

He listed them. The fourth man was me. I had a great sense of relief. During the trip I had a number of opportunities to speak in churches and in street meetings. Some of the churches had survived under communism. I saw the manifestation of their great faith under persecution that I had only read about in history books.

I saw meetings where people believed in and acted on the Word of God from 1 Corinthians chapter 14. It says, "Let the prophets speak, two or three; and if another has the Word of the Lord, let the first sit down, and him stand up."

This dynamic actually occurred as a regular pattern in church meetings. As many as four or five often spoke, and the pastor of the church was most unique in that he was not identifiable at the meeting. He was simply one of the men sitting in the congregation. One could gather from small clues regarding the way he interacted with the meeting that he was the pastor. He truly wasn't there to be seen of men. He was a shepherd watching over the sheep.

Singing erupted spontaneously from the congregation of three hundred people. They had no song leaders or worship team in front. They had no musical instruments. Music came forth from individuals sprinkled throughout the meeting room who had unction from the Holy Spirit. It was a beautiful experience. I might add, when our team drove into the small unpaved parking lots in front of the churches, we were initially shocked that the parking lots were empty. Our leader informed us that the church was packed full. He was right! Everyone had walked, some for many hours.

We also visited a church more like the American pattern with about six hundred present. This particular church had a pastor who was very strong-handed. Nothing happened that he didn't direct. He told them when to stand and sit, and operated more in the mode of the Greek Orthodox Church. I was assigned to speak in that particular meeting. The Lord gave me a strong word. As it happened, this church building had become an idol in the eyes of the congregation. The reason it was so important to them, was that prior to the fall Communism, they had built it illegally. At one point, the Communist government sent bulldozers to demolish the church.

The people, in an act of passive resistance, stood in a circle around the church requiring that the bulldozers bulldoze them first before the building. As it happened, the men driving the bulldozers refused to drive through the crowd and the building was saved. That activity preceded those that stood in front of the wall in Bucharest that actually were killed. They were Christians who said, "Enough is enough. We can't take any more of the oppression from this Communist regime."

In the latter instance, the machine guns came out and hundreds of people died, and outrage over the deaths was the catalyst for the revolution. Within days of their deaths, Ceausescu was assassinated and a new era had begun. The protection of the church by the people was very significant, but the people had turned the building into an idol.

I spoke a strong word and asked them to check it against the Scripture. I showed them that the true church was not a building made of

He Inclined His Ear

wood and stones, but it was made of living stones, jointly fit together. The temple of the Holy Ghost was not a construction of man, but a construction of God. We are the tabernacle of God, not the building. At a certain point, I found myself prophesying that most of the people in the congregation would not be able to hear or understand the Word of the Lord because of the idolatry and love of the building that was in their hearts. Then I pointed to the balcony where a number of children were sitting, and said, "But the children who are hearing this message, they will have their eyes opened, and they will hear the Word of the Lord. It will affect their walk with Jesus in the future years."

At the end of the meeting, the brother who was interpreting the message fell into my arms with weeping. He was overcome by the clarity of the Word of the Lord, and he knew in his heart of hearts that God had spoken to that congregation. Months later, we received the gift of Angie Filimon from Romania who came to live with us at age 12. She became our adopted daughter. She eventually went to a Bible college in Rhode Island. Attending the college at the same time, there was a young girl from Romania who had been a friend of Angie's. When I met this young girl, now a young woman, she was able to tell me that she was one of the young people in that balcony. She had heard the Word of the Lord that day.

W. Stephen Keel

Chapter 11: For What Purpose?

The choreography of God is frequently very difficult to understand. Some things that happen are hard to receive. This happened to me on more than one occasion. One day I drove to town in a vehicle that had been donated to us by a brother in the Lord from North Carolina. The vehicle was remarkable because it met the needs of space to carry my family and was a far better vehicle than I could afford at the time. I was still the volunteer chaplain at Blanch Prison, and we were still living on a very restricted income. It was so restricted that when I took Ezekiel, my son, to a restaurant, I bought him a milkshake. I didn't have enough money to buy one for me, but I was in a state of joy that I had enough to buy one for him.

He finished the milkshake and we drove across town. I intended to have a mechanic take a look at the transmission to verify that it was working okay. It is necessary to understand that during this trip, I had no iota of bitterness in my heart over the fact that I was penniless. In fact, the opposite existed; I was quite excited that I had enough money to be a blessing to my son. There was joy in my heart as I drove across the city. We pulled up to a particular intersection, and I looked to the left, and I looked to the right.

The sun was at a place in the sky that was quite blinding, and unfortunately I turned away too soon. When I pulled into the intersection, a car was traveling 55 mph from the blinding spot of the sun. It smashed into the passenger's side of our car where my only son was sitting. It was startling to say the least, but as it turned out, the only damage was to the two vehicles. My car was totaled. I know that bad things happen to bad people, but I was walking in the Spirit experiencing the joy of my salvation, when out of the sunlight came a rushing vehicle that totaled my car.

"Oh, Lord, What is this all about?"

Before long the tow truck arrived to take our car to the junk yard. I would be negotiating for the few hundred salvageable dollars of value left in the car.

He Inclined His Ear

I ended up spending several hours at the junk yard. During those few hours, the owner of the junk yard began talking to me and sharing some of the details of his life. I probed a bit and I discovered that he had been an enthusiastic Christian who fifteen years prior had fallen into the sin of adultery. He had blamed his fall on Christians and on the church. Since then, he had walked in bitterness and hatred toward the Christian church. During those next few hours, the Lord granted me grace to speak into his life in such a way that his hunger for God was rekindled. It was really a significant conversation.

At the end of the conversation, I received from the Lord that He, in His love for this man, had spent my car as the price to get into the presence of this man, to speak these endearing words of life. Many years later, I learned that the man had in fact returned to God's fold and was following Jesus. That was a confirmation that I heard from God when He told me that He had spent my vehicle as the price to turn the man back to God.

The choreography of God is truly a beautiful thing to behold. When my oldest daughter Rose of Sharon was preparing to graduate from the University of Virginia, I found myself in a financial situation where it was possible for me to take a vacation at the beach with my family. In years past, the amount of money that I dedicated to this vacation would have been a tenth of my income for an entire year. I sensed that the Lord would be pleased if we would pull away from work and go off to enjoy a week at Nags Head beach. The problem was that my daughter was a member of the Fellowship of Christian Athletes, a campus organization, and unbeknownst to me, she had made arrangements to travel with them for a weekend to some beach some place on the very same week.

When I called her on the phone to give her the good news that our family was taking the trip, she said, "Gee, Dad, that's the same week that I have already committed to go to the beach with my college friends. You know what great fellowship I have with these people, and I feel a need to be with them."

This was distressing to me because I had never had the ability to take my family on a vacation at the beach, and now my oldest daughter whom I particularly wanted to draw back into my arms with the rest of the family wasn't going to be available.

I asked her, "What's the location of the place where you are going to be staying?"

You guessed it....Nags Head, North Carolina. The group was staying five blocks away from the house I had rented for our own family for the same week!. The Lord in his sovereign oversight of our lives arranged for my daughter to be with her friends and with her family on the same week for a vacation. Not only did He make it possible for us to be together as a family, but He also gave us the opportunity to get to know a lot of her friends. It was an exhilarating time.

I had made a commitment to teach my family a daily Bible study on the subject of "fear". I wanted to talk about the fear of God, the fear of man, and the fear of failure. I wanted to open up the Scriptures in a deep way. I used the lead verse to hook into the Bible study from Proverbs 28:1 that says, "The wicked flee when no man pursues, but the righteous are as bold as lions."

(I had no idea what impact that would have on my five year-old daughter Nancy Stephanie, but many years later when she was traveling in the ancient market bazaars of Istanbul by herself, she reminded me that I had taught her that the righteous are as bold as lions. She used that as protection for running around the market place.)

Well, I organized the Bible study every day at a specific time for studying this subject of "fear". On the second day at the beach, my wife and I walked along the beach with our little clutch of children. The beach was deserted except for one young man who was standing with his feet in the water looking out at the ocean. The Lord stirred my heart and I approached him. He told me that he also was a graduate of the University of Virginia (UVA). Curiously his trip to the beach had nothing to do with the Fellowship of Christian Athletes. He had not been associated with them at UVA because he was a profound atheist. He was an intelligent man. He was an Echols Scholar. His academic achievements had put him at the university, tuition free, for four years, and he wasn't required to take any of the prerequisites for graduation. He was allowed to take any course he liked at any level at any time. He designed his own curricula.

He Inclined His Ear

He had just graduated. The Lord showed me that his standing in the water and looking at the ocean was the result of the fact that his four years at the university had not answered the deep questions that he had sought after. I simply spoke to him, "It's clear to me that you have not yet received the answers that are stirring deep inside your heart regarding where we came from and what this all means, or your purpose in life. Let me tell you about Jesus."

I stood in the ocean with him and preached the Gospel while my family stayed on the shore a few hundred yards away. He needed only about thirty minutes of explanation because the Holy Spirit had been preparing him. I was just the spiritual midwife who had been sent for the moment of delivery.

He gladly received Jesus Christ as his Lord and Savior and became a member of our family for the rest of the week, attending the Bible studies that we had on the subject of fear. I saw the hand of God, the divine choreography functioning for my family and for the benefit of this young man. I don't know where he is today, but I believe that I will meet him in heaven, and he will rejoice that we had an opportunity to speak together on the beach that day.

Rose of Sharon's graduation from the university as the second youngest student in her class brought us to a position that every parent dreads. We found ourselves turning her over to her own life. She was outside of our world of control and influence. She was so far away! Because of her degree in chemistry, she had been granted an interview and had gained a position working in a laboratory at Johns Hopkins University in Baltimore, Maryland. With the excitement of graduation and trip to the beach, she had not gotten everything together for the move to Baltimore. She needed a place for long-term residency and had no idea where to look. After she arrived in Baltimore, she called me on the phone and said, "Dad, I know where I am working, but I don't where I am going to live."

I said, "One thing I know. You are not there randomly. I believe that God has a purpose for you being there, and the most fulfilling purposes in Baltimore will come as you make contact with the body of Christ. You will find Christians and develop relationships with them, and through that will come the provision that you need. So, let's pray...Father, in the name of Jesus, I ask You to give Rose of Sharon a connection with the body of Christ in Baltimore, Maryland. Please use this connection as a source of provision and protection for her as she stays there and pursues her new career. Father, I thank You in the name of Jesus."

She said, "I have got to go now. It is time for work."

She hung up the phone. Later she called me back and said, "Dad, you are not going to believe what happened. I stepped out of the phone booth, and I saw a man standing on the corner preaching the Gospel to the people passing by. I walked up to him and said I was sorry to interrupt his preaching, but is there some way I can get in contact with you after work? And he said yes and gave me his business card. After work, I called him, and he and his wife invited me to come and stay in their home while I am living here in Baltimore."

The Lord answered that prayer virtually instantaneously. She lived the next number of months in their home. It was a beautiful experience.

Chapter 12: The Abnormal Can Be Normal

I hope you are seeing from these illustrations how a "nobody" can be a "somebody" in the body of Christ by simply hearing the voice of God and obeying it, to be consciously aware of His presence, and to acknowledge the divine choreography. The purpose of these stories is to show how God invades our daily lives. He is a part of our daily existence even though the things that are occurring don't seem to have any broader purpose or value than an insignificant event ....things like my wife needing a parking space in downtown Richmond for a 15 passenger van full of little kids. Something like that can be difficult to handle with one-way streets, time constraints and getting children herded to and from events. She simply prayed for a parking place so that she could be on time. She located the place where they were to attend a meeting on small-farm agriculture. A car pulled out and she was able to effortlessly pull in with the large van.

I really believe that this type of interaction with the Holy Spirit is to be a normal part of Christian life. We should be talking to Jesus and listening to Him, following Him in what appears to be the mundane aspects of our lives.

In the year 2000, we were blessed with an opportunity to travel to England to visit our daughter Rebecca who was both having a birthday and a spring break from the University of Bath. As it happened, three of us went: my wife, Nancy Stephanie, and I. One of the reasons we were able to go was that in our business, we use credit cards for purchases of saleable inventory, so we had accumulated airplanes points. The tickets were paid by for by those points. My wife scheduled it so that she traveled two days in advance of Nancy Stephanie and me. She actually arrived in Bath on Rebecca's birthday and waited for us to arrive later.

Rebecca had sent me an email describing where she lived, directions on how to get there, and a telephone number,... everything that was necessary for us to find her. I received the email and read the first paragraph of it to be sure that I had the right email. I printed it out but didn't pay attention to the rest of the email until we had rented a car in Gatwick and had driven to the city of Bath. At a certain point the directions stopped, and I realized that the email had been truncated. The last part of the email never reached me, and I had no more directions how to get to Rebecca's home. The information that was truncated was her actual address and phone number.

What an unusual predicament to be sitting in a rented car coming into Bath, England. My wife and daughter were there, and I had not a clue how I would be able to find them. It was a holiday, so even the university was closed and couldn't help us. I said to Nancy Stephanie, "Clearly, this is one of those predicaments where we haven't any other resources,... no way of making contact. Evidently what we have to do is pray."

So I prayed, "Father, in the name of Jesus, You have brought us this far by faith, and I believe that You can take us the rest of the way. You will make it possible for us to find my wife and my daughter. I commit myself to going in the general direction from the last information on the email. I am expecting You to reveal to us as we drive exactly where we need to drive in the city."

As I prayed this prayer, my wife was in my daughter's apartment, which was about two blocks off the main street in a narrow dead-end alley. It was obscured by several turns and trees. No one would know it was there unless you lived there, but Nancy, my wife, had a leading from the Lord. In her spirit she received that it was close to time that we were supposed to be arriving. She thought that we might miss the turn into the alley way.

So as we were praying, she was walking out the door several blocks away toward an intersection. She arrived only minutes before we drove by. I looked out the window and saw her. She looked at the traffic in the street and saw us in the rented car.

Nancy Stephanie and I said, ""Praise the Lord! Thank You Jesus for answering our prayer!"

My wife simply said, "I really expected you to drive by."

And we were there! God is the Divine Choreographer. He hears our prayer and He directs our steps.

He Inclined His Ear

Walking in the spirit and realizing that God, in fact, really has directed our steps is a total and normal activity for any individual who has bowed his knee to the lordship of Christ. One of the gratifying aspects of this walk is that there is no condemnation to those who are in Christ Jesus. It is not necessary to be uptight or overly-anxious about whether or not you are hearing the voice of God properly. The Lord is in the resurrection business. If you mess up, He is able to fix it, so we don't have to walk in fear. We can walk in faith.

I am particularly energized by the Scripture in John chapter 10 that talks about hearing the voice of God. He says that He is the Good Shepherd, and His sheep hear and know His voice. He continues by telling us that His sheep go in and out freely.

Many years ago I received that this means that we don't have to walk in condemnation or frustration or fear over whether or not we are following Jesus as He is leading us. We are just sheep. We can go into the fold and be close to the Shepherd, or we can go out of the fold and wander about in the fields. We can partake of whatever we encounter as we move about. The key is that we go in and out freely. Whether we are close to the Shepherd, listening directly to His voice, or whether we are wandering into the activities of the day, He is still the Shepherd. He is still watching over us and will keep us wherever we are. Great freedom! There is great freedom in that!

This was more or less the state of mind I was in, when the Lord spoke to me that I was to make a record of these events and to write this book. I received direction to write this book when I was in Chicago visiting my daughter Rose of Sharon and her family. My wife and I went to their church service and later to their church picnic in the afternoon. We played baseball. At least we tried, but there weren't enough players to make a team. Four or five of us went to the field anyway. We were pitching and hitting the ball. It was good fellowship.

Typically at church picnics of this type a visitor assumes that everyone else is a Christian and a member of the church. Fellowship was flowing among groups of women, and the children were running about playing with each other. I made that assumption that all appeared "saved" and happy, though I really didn't know anybody.

W. Stephen Keel

When we got back to the food area, one of the guys who had been playing baseball was in line ahead of me...not uncommon, not unreasonable...but part of the divine choreography. I looked at his right hand, and I saw that it was badly wounded. Without giving a great deal of thought to it, but merely walking in the mindset that the Lord had given me with young criminals in the past, I asked him, "Where did you get those injuries to your hand? Was it in a barroom brawl?"

When I said that, he looked at me with big blue eyes and said, "Yes, as a matter of fact, it was. I nearly lost my hand. I have had several operations trying to save it."

I said, "If you were in a barroom brawl, chances are you have other interesting things going on in your life. Why don't we step out of line and have a little conversation. Tell me about yourself."

He began to describe how he had been running from God and how he had fallen into deep sin. He felt that there was no way possible that he would ever be able to be restored again to God. Following the barroom brawl, he had suffered deep pain and emotional disturbance. Even so, he had an encounter with God. God told him that He loved him and wanted him to have an abundant life in Jesus.

As the young man shared his testimony with me, I could see how tentative he was regarding all of it. He had obviously had a deep encounter with the Holy Spirit, but he was still on shaky ground. He was uncertain of the significance of what had happened in his life. I was able to speak to him and explain that he was a royal priest and a minister of reconciliation, that God was the God of his entire life....not just when he was "good". In the economy of God, nothing is wasted. In fact, the most useful things that would come out of all his experience would be the comfort he had received from God. He could then take that comfort to comfort others. God had commissioned him to do this, and he would be used mightily of the Lord to bring others to the Lord who felt it was impossible to be restored to a relationship in Christ.

The conversation was clearly ordained of God, and the man was mightily ministered to and blessed. After the conversation ended and my wife and I discussed it, my wife pointed out how "forward" it was to speak to someone at a church picnic and suggest that the problems in his life were caused by a fight in a bar. She pointed out that this wasn't the first time I had walked in that boldness. She was impressed by the results of it and told me she believed that I was sup-supposed to begin to record my interactions with God. I could present them to Christians so that they too could be granted some of the freedom and liberty that I had in Christ. They too could have experiences walking in the excitement that comes from hearing the voice of God and obeying it.

She also added as an after-thought, that not many people at the picnic were talking to the man. Maybe they knew of his troubles or instinctively felt he had a troubled life, and they didn't know what to say to him. I would suggest that if you are willing and listening, God may tell you to speak to anyone at any time.

W. Stephen Keel

Chapter 13: The Divine Choreography

At the moment, I am seated in the living room of my brother Paul Chapman. Paul has experienced a debilitating stroke that left him paralyzed on the left side of his body. A former editor of the Springville Journal, he is interrupting my narrative to ask questions. My mother is dying in the next room. I had hoped to dictate some of these stories so that she could listen in, but she has already drifted far away from us. We are waiting for the end.

We have a small Christmas tree on the table to my right. A wood fire is protecting us from the cold winter night in upstate New York. I am reflecting on things that have happened in my life, that at least in my opinion, reveal the hand of God. There is a great controversy in many people's hearts, as to whether God really gets involved in people's lives. Many times when people say that they heard something from God, they are accused of being a lunatic or a liar, so it is my desire to present just the facts of what happened, and let you make a decision for yourself as to whether I am a lunatic, a liar, or hopefully one to whom the Creator has spoken directly and personally.

This particular story begins on a day when I was having a fight with a computer. I had been in the computer business for 18 years. The Internet was emerging. Technology was advancing. Someone had given me a notebook computer and asked me to hook it up to the Internet. At that particular time in history, it wasn't very easy to do. There were problems with drivers for the modems and software that needed to be downloaded that was appropriate for that particular Internet service provider. I spent two and a half hours trying to make this computer talk to the Internet.

I like to say that I had a fight with the computer and I won, but what came out of it was more interesting than I could have possibly expected. At the end of the fight, I felt as if I had burned a deep dark hole in eternity. The two and a half hours I had just spent appeared to be a victory, but in my heart I felt as if it were a meaningless, empty waste of time. Surely there were more important things that I could do with my time than mess with this computer. I did what seemed to be a reasonable thing to do…I prayed.

I said, "Lord, would You please give me something else to do with my time that has more significance than what I was just doing these last few hours."

Later that night, Nancy and I were visiting friends who had a house on a lake nearby. At the end of the evening, we were standing on the front porch, and I mentioned to them the dilemma I had experienced earlier in the day. I told them how I had prayed for the Lord to give me something else to do. They said, "Why don't we pray again right now. Perhaps the Lord will speak to you."

So we prayed. While we were praying, I heard what is called in the Bible, "a still small voice," and the still small voice said, "Build chicken coops".

At the end of the prayer, I told my wife and the people I was with that God had spoken to me, that I was to build chicken coops. This was a rather surprising instruction to be given to a person who had in recent years sold two to three million dollars' worth of computers annually.

I pondered why I might have been told to build chicken coops, recalling that I had been in England several months earlier. As we toured the countryside staying at various Bed and Breakfasts, I had eaten eggs with beautiful deep yellow yokes. These eggs tasted remarkably different from the eggs I was used to buying in the grocery stores in the United States.

Having grown up in a rural community and having had chickens as a child, I knew that one of the reasons those eggs were so good was that they came from "free range" chickens.

Backing up just a little; as we toured the British countryside, I had a problem with the definition of "free range eggs". Here was the problem: I saw a lot of signs that said "Free Range Eggs." As a businessman, I had no idea how they could be giving away free eggs, but as an English major, I resolved the problem. The signs were referring to "free range" eggs, not "free" range eggs. The farmer wanted their potential customers to know that their eggs had the deep

W. Stephen Keel

yellow yokes and firm whites from chickens that were allowed to "range" around the farm eating bugs and fresh grass.

Twenty years previously, I had seen a front page article in "The Mother Earth News" describing a chicken tractor. A chicken tractor lets you move chickens in a cage without a floor. The chickens eat grass and bugs, making healthy eggs. I had tried twice to build one, but I wasn't successful.

My ensuing conversation with the Lord went about like this; "If You want me to build chicken coops, then hopefully You don't want me to do something really stupid."

I had learned as an entrepreneur, that if a person wants to pursue a business, it would be best to do something that someone else is already doing successfully, and just do it as well or better! This is a pathway to success. I had also learned that God opens His hand and closes His hand, causing an individual to prosper or perish. Hoping that this direction came with an open hand, I said, "Okay, Lord, if this is You speaking to me, then You will show me somebody that is already building chicken coops and doing very well. If I find that person, then I will know that it is You speaking to me, telling me to build chicken coops."

Many times I have been asked the question, "How did you know that the still small voice was the voice of God?"

I have a biblical reference that helped me understand what this is all about. In chapter 32 of Jeremiah, we see the Prophet Jeremiah in a prison cell. He heard a voice from God that said, "Your cousin Hanamel will come to visit you and ask you to buy a piece of land that he owns."

Jeremiah was concerned about doing that, because at that very time, King Nebuchadnezzar had surrounded the city of Jerusalem, and it appeared that the city would surrender to him in a matter of days. All of the real estate in the area was about to become totally worthless. Jeremiah was troubled about making a real estate investment.

God said to him, "Behold, I am the Lord, the God of all flesh. Is there anything too hard for Me?" Shortly after that, his cousin came to visit him and offered to sell him the land. Jeremiah agreed, paid for the land and sealed the transaction with witnesses. Then God spoke again and said that in 70 years, when the children of Israel return from Babylonian captivity, the land that you purchased will become valuable again.

After Jeremiah's cousin left, he declared, "Now I know that I heard the voice of God because my cousin came and offered me the land for sale."

This is an example revealing how subsequent events prove the validity of the experience of hearing the voice of God. I have experienced this validation in the chicken coop business.

My wife thought it was outrageous to stop selling computers and to start building chicken coops. The night I received the still small voice regarding building chicken coops, I logged into the Internet. Almost immediately, I found a man in England who had been building chicken coops for over 20 years. He had distributors in five countries and his business was healthy. This information satisfied the requirement that the Lord would show me someone else that was successful. This helped me believe that I had actually heard the voice of God.

My first response was to call England and to attempt to strike a deal for selling coops. But, God didn't tell me to "sell" chicken coops. He told me to "build" and sell chicken coops. My negotiations with the manufacturer in England fell through. Working with him was not a viable business opportunity. I began thinking and praying about what kind of chicken coop would people in the United States need.

I designed a chicken coop for people who had grown up in the country, gone to college, gotten a job in the city and made enough money to move back to the country. They wanted their children to have the experience of going to the chicken house to gather eggs. I knew that they needed to be able to go away on weekends, so I designed the coops that didn't require constant attention. The owners could go away for several days, and the eggs and chickens would be protected. I added various other features to eventually create a successful business with national exposure and acceptance.

The chicken coop business was the beginning of an evolving activity. About a year after I began building these chicken coops, I received a phone call from a man in Florida, who told me that he was participating in a nutrition rescue program in the Dominican Republic. Paul Rahill was working with a private foundation, funding activities in a small village. Their ongoing medical mission and associated research indicated that if starving children could eat one egg every day of their lives, the nutritional benefits in the egg were enough to reverse malnutrition. They had decided that they wanted members of the community to have chicken coops.

The question has been asked, how did this man who wanted eggs for the people in the Dominican Republic find me? As it happens, I may have been the only person in the United States that God had spoken to how to build and sell chicken coops. For a short period of time, my website was literally the only website in North America offering backyard chicken coops for sale. When Paul Rahill began looking for chicken coops for the Dominican Republic families, he found me online right away.

I told him that I didn't think it was reasonable for my coops to be used in the Dominican Republic. I told him I had designed them for people who had disposable income. In other words, I was making expensive chicken coops. Paul said he was not as concerned about the cost as he was about rescuing these people from the nutritional crisis. I told him that as much as I would like to sell 50 coops, I didn't believe that my chicken coops were right for the people in the Dominican Republic.

I made a suggestion, "If you will buy me an airplane ticket and travel with me to the Dominican Republic, we will visit the village where you want to put the coops. We will walk about and look at the homes the people live in. We will consider their economic condition, and we will seek the Lord, and perhaps He will give us an idea of how to meet the needs of these particular people."

Paul said, "Okay, let me call you back."

He called back three days later. We set a date to travel, and He bought me an airplane ticket. For eight days, we walked on the end of the earth among a people who had no resources. There was no Post Office, police department, electricity or telephone. These people were living on the edge of the earth in what I can only describe as "surprising poverty".

He Inclined His Ear

There was a small problem regarding our walkabout. It had to do with the fact that I was a 55-year old fat guy, and Paul was a 40-year old that had run in the Boston Marathon the previous week. He didn't tell me about how fit he was until the end of the trip. We spent most of the time walking about the mountains with me huffing and puffing.

I only mention this to say that the joy of the Lord was my strength on this trip. On the third day, when we had hiked about eight miles, I was about ready to "die" from climbing the extremely steep hills. I decided to test the principle that teaches us that the joy of the Lord is our strength. I did this by singing a little song that I had learned as a young Christian. The song simply says, "The joy of the Lord is my strength."

It was quite a challenge to sing out loud and climb the steep trails at the same time, but as I sang that verse over and over again, I became invigorated to the point that at the end of a nine-mile march, I was the first person to walk back into the village where we were staying. Jesus had inclined His ear unto me and given me supernatural strength.

As we were walking among these families, talking to them individually, looking at their circumstances, analyzing their plight, I received in my mind and in my heart, an idea that would make it possible for them to get the one egg a day that was required.

It was clear that although they had chickens, the main reason that their chickens weren't laying eggs was that they didn't have quality feed. The reason they didn't have quality feed is that the owners didn't have money. Reflecting on technology that I had learned from Joel Salatin in Virginia, I realized that I could build a chicken house that would house not only chickens, but also house pigs. The pigs could be sold at market to raise cash and the cash could be used to buy feed. The chickens could eat high quality feed and produce an egg a day.

For the Dominican Republic project, the foundation gave the people in the community the money necessary to buy chickens, pigs and feed to produce eggs. Within six months, we installed a small cage that we called a "Foodspa." In it were two small pigs and 10 chickens. The people in the community were astounded to discover that a chicken could lay an egg nearly every day. They didn't know that this was possible. Of course, it is very possible. This is what makes raising chickens in the USA profitable.

The villagers didn't realize that a pig could grow as rapidly as what they saw with their own eyes. They often took seven years to raise a pig. They used the pigs as a "money market" fund. They slaughtered the pig for special events like a wedding or a funeral. They never viewed the pigs as something they could raise, kill and sell. When they saw the small pigs that we brought into their community grow to market size within a mere 14 weeks, they were astounded. They simply didn't know it was possible.

As I was pursuing this activity, making multiple trips to the Dominican Republic and sending an employee of mine to build and install the Foodspas, I realized there was a major problem….it had to do with how their cash was managed. I saw money from the foundation handed out rather liberally at various times with no receipts being given. There was little or no accountability. No way could a truly profitable business emerge following these practices. I saw the need for agricultural technology, but I also understood clearly that they needed a mechanism for managing their money, so that it wouldn't be lost through theft and mismanagement.

One of the reasons I was sensitive to the needs of the people in the Dominican Republic is that since 1986, I had been traveling to the country of Haiti which is on the same island as the Dominican Republic. Graft and corruption were very prevalent in Haiti in the marketplace, in business, etc. It was in Haiti that the Lord had arranged for me to have a radio program. How the radio program came into existence is another story where I heard the voice of the Lord.

Jerry Austin, a member of our little house church, told me that he had received a mailing from someone in North Carolina who was promoting Christian radio in the country of Mexico. He thought that I should call Michael Escalante in Wilmington, North Carolina. Michael and I chatted and discovered our mutual interest in the sharing of the Gospel over the radio. That call changed the entire direction of my life. Shortly after that first call, Michael said he was going to attend a Christian Radio Broadcasters Conference in Acapulco, Mexico, and he invited me to go with him.

He Inclined His Ear

(This is another story unfolding parallel to my meeting Magdalena Latorre, the future translator for my Spanish radio program "Un Proverbio al Dia.") While I was in Acapulco, I sought to discover if anyone in Mexico was interested in the Foodspa project. I was introduced to a man from the University of Mexico who was an agronomist and a Christian pastor. He was also in the pork industry on a national level in Mexico. He said that I should attend a conference in Chiapas, Mexico that was focused on "How the Church Should Respond to Poverty in Mexico."

Within a few months, Gary Gaddy, Nuel West, and I were in Tuxtla Gutiérrez, Chiapas, Mexico. We were greeted by an 88 year-old man who also hears the voice of God. He had pastored a church of 5000 members over a period of 40 years. Their work extended to more than 240 small churches around the state of Chiapas. He was known in the community as "The Prophet". The night we arrived he learned of our mission to introduce chickens, pigs and banking for the unbanked. Jesus Castelazo laid hands on me and said, "Thus saith the Lord: this project will be a great benefit to the nation of Mexico, and I, the Lord, God, have commissioned you to bring this to My people."

It was startling to have someone be that emphatic about why we were there. In less than four days, they arranged a meeting with over 200 pastors to give us an opportunity to present our project. We began the process of interviewing potential candidates for receiving chickens, pigs and our financial services system in Mexico. A local pastor received the role of manager for the project. He interviewed 110 families, providing their names, their ages, their children, and their photographs. I was able to put this information on a website and to begin the process of designing a special coop for people lacking a modest income.

The next three years were focused on "witty inventions." I had read in the book of Proverbs that it's the king's privilege to discover or to invent. Seeing myself as one of the King's kids, I received that as a member of the royal family, this proverb applied to me. I am free to discover and invent. One of the beauties of discovering and inventing is that not all that is invented is profitable. I made many things that simply didn't work, but I did endeavor to hear the voice of the Lord in everything I did. I thank the Lord for an indulgent wife. She stood by

W. Stephen Keel

patiently as I spent much needed grocery money on complicated inventions that simply flunked.

My brother-in-law Paul was an editor in a local newspaper, and he had the job of writing stories. He explained to me that one of the ways he found inspiration for writing the stories was that he thought of a "lead" to the story. Many times the "lead" came to him early in the morning, so he would get out of bed and jot down the idea. When he had the "lead," he had the story.

That is the way I developed chicken coops for three years. I would face a problem; I would seek an answer, and frequently I would awake at three a.m. and have an idea. I would jot down that idea and began working on it. Some of the ideas took several months to discover their value, but the process fine-tuned my ability to hear the voice of God and to be led by the Spirit.

There is a relationship between doing and knowing. Jesus says in John 7:17, "Anyone who wants to do the will of God will know whether My teaching is from God or is merely My own."

Virtually everything I have learned about hearing the voice of God has been connected to my willingness to do what I heard Him say. Until you act on the still small voice, you are left in a constant state of paralysis by analysis.

"Did He speak? Was that God?" Often the only way to know is to act on what you have heard.

I understand clearly that one of the best things a person can do in trying to follow God is to fail, because a failure is a very "positive" signal. There is no better way to get a clear understanding of how messed up we are. I learned because Jesus is the Redeemer that He is in the resurrection business. I do not have to fear failure. I can spend three or four months, or three or four years on an invention. Often, my wife looked at some of the contraptions I built, and said, "Wow, I don't feel good about this one."

One "great mistake" invention was called the "Pig-Powered Pump." The pigs would walk up a ramp to get food. Their weight would cause the ramp to drop down about two feet articulating cylinders that pumped pond water. The pond water was used to clean the system.

He Inclined His Ear

My idea was that hungry pigs would learn to walk the ramp to get food. I soon discovered that big pigs bullied the others away from the ramp. They also skidded whenever the ramp was wet and could break a leg easily. I changed the system many times and attempted to refine the mechanics over many months, but the project failed.

I had told my wife that I didn't have any choice. I had to follow my understanding of where I was going in this phase of the project. This was a huge mistake because Proverbs chapter 3 clearly states that we are not to lean on our own understanding. We all have to discern the difference between following our own understanding and walking in obedience to His preceding Word. Because of my willfulness, the best way I could make this distinction was to fail. I have embraced these failures as valuable lessons in the process of learning how to acknowledge God in all my ways.

My friend Michael Escalante moved to Mexico for a period of time. The Lord led him by the Spirit to meet some very interesting people. One of the people he met was the director of an organization called Financier Rural. Jaime Almonte has a Ph.D. in global economics. As Director, he was responsible for technical training and assistance for loan programs to rural farmers such as "Help for the Hungry" (HFTH), an organization that I started for feeding the rural poor, using Foodspas in the Dominican Republic.

When he learned of my project, he invited me to come to his home. I spent six weeks in his gracious home on a mountain overlooking Mexico City. We went to church on Sundays. I preached and he acted as an interpreter. Every day I went with him to his office. He introduced me to some of the very powerful people in the nation of Mexico. One day I ate lunch with one of the richest men in Mexico. I sat at a table in a restaurant next to the Secretary of the Treasury. I discovered the relationship between the favor of God and the favor of man.

Financiera Rural contracted me to do an engineering study. They paid me $44,000 to study the potential value of my ideas for Mexico. This was the first step toward the fulfillment of the prophecy that was spoken over me by Jesus Castelazo in Chiapas.

Financiera Rural is an organization with politically powerful people, some of which were set directly against implementing my project. There existed a mixture of powerful people interested in seeing HFTH succeed and powerful people interested in seeing it stopped. Health issues and bird flu issues were paraded out against us.

I worked on a Saturday afternoon to draft a response to the concerns that had been raised. About 10am, I walked from the guest house to the main house to use the printer in Dr. Almonte's office. As I walked into the house, I met the father and mother of a friend of Dr. Almonte's son as they were walking out the door. We exchanged greetings and I learned that the man I nearly missed seeing was a nationally respected research scientist. After hearing details about my project, he gladly endorsed it and provided a signed, written explanation of why our project was sound science. He and I both recognized that the Lord had directed our steps. Instead of leaving, we spent the next two hours enthusiastically discussing the exciting ways that Jesus had revealed Himself to each of us.

The fact that I often receive enabling grace is evidence that I was being led by the Spirit. At times, when I thought I could not possibly go on, I found a small amount of energy that enabled me to take the next step. That next step often proved to be more beneficial than I could have ever believed possible.

The end result of one and half year's work was a declaration from Financiera Rural that they were NOT going to pursue my project. They didn't believe that it was possible due to many factors: the price of corn, the price of pork and other details. All along I had said, "Well, Lord, if You really want me to do this, make it possible for it to move ahead, and if You don't want me to do it, please stop it so that I can be delivered from all the effort, time and money I am investing."

In spite of this apparent hiatus on the project, I received grace to continue to pursue it. Through prayer, discussions and involvement with other people, I was given the insight to create the organization called Wel-Fi, a private online banking system for the poor. For God to get glory there has to be some form of "gory" present. The people who see the greatest obstacles have the greatest victories.

He Inclined His Ear

In February of 2007, on the day when I accomplished the completion of the engineering study for Financiera Rural, I experienced a day of unique satisfaction. I had completed the project. The completed report had been freshly printed that very afternoon. I was also satisfied that the chicken coop business God had instructed me to start was quite successful. I had finished manufacturing about $30,000 worth of inventory getting ready for spring sales. On the way back from the press where I had printed copies of the report for Mexico, I stopped by the shop and simply enjoyed the order and organization of everything I saw. I was fulfilled. The date was February 28, 2007.

I went to bed without another thought until someone pulled into my driveway about 10pm and began honking their horn and flashing their lights. Then, they disappeared down the driveway. My wife got out of bed and went downstairs to check on this very noisy car. As she entered the dining room she saw an eerie orange light reflected against the wall. She went into the living room to see where it was coming from, only to discover the chicken coop shop was bathed in a blaze of fire. We went outside and saw that all I had worked to build over the last five years engulfed in flames.

She called 911, but they never answered the phone. Finally she called a member of the fire department that we knew personally. During the next hour, several fire departments came, and several hundred people watched the coop inventory, all the tools and the shop go up in flames. Not only was my source of income gone, but I had also lost the prototypes of my HFTH project. Fortunately, God had already spoken to my wife and me a very important message which is another story you will read later.

The message was that God had never taken anything away from us, except that He had given us back something better than whatever He had taken away. As we stood and watched the building burn, we held forth in faith the promise of God that He would replace it. We had very little insurance on the building because carpentry shops are big fire hazards and the insurance premiums are very high.

I had grace to worship the Lord as the building burned. One of the nice things about something this bad is you don't have to think about how others think about you. The result is that I was not the least bit embarrassed to simply sing praises to God and to enjoy the presence of Jesus in the midst of the fire. My wife and I knew the Lord was doing something. She had had a troubling dream two nights before where she saw a sky-blue letter "L" and a small red thread lying across the front of it. She asked the Lord the meaning of it and received that the "L" stood for the Lord, but she didn't get an answer for the red thread. Only after the fire did she remember the dream and figure out that the red thread was the fire.

The fire destroyed everything. In a few days a good friend, Kelly Rodgers, came to me and said, "God has spoken to me and several men in the community, and we are going to rebuild your shop."

This was very important because the insurance on the building was negligible. The idea that God would speak to men and tell them to rebuild my building was wonderful. Had they not heard that voice, I am not sure that I had faith to begin rebuilding at that particular time. By grasping the faith that they had exercised and by receiving the gifts and free labor that these men provided, a new building was constructed within three months.

Not only did I end up with a new building, but George Everding, a man I had met only casually, received from the Lord an intense interest in helping me to rebuild the shop. He showed up at my place on a daily basis declaring that he was only there to be a servant of Jesus. He had his own business; he owned two Subway restaurants with a large number of employees, but his work was such that he could take off from work fairly large blocks of time and present himself to me at my location. As we were rebuilding, he would tell me stories about his life. One of the things I learned was that his son was going to play in a home school basketball tournament on a Saturday night in Winston Salem, North Carolina.

When he told me that, I felt an urgency from the Lord, a leading from God, a still small voice that said, "Go to the basketball game."

I told Nancy that we were supposed to go to that basketball game and watch some people play that we didn't know. We would not know any of the people at the game except George and his wife. I had not even met his son, but I had a strong sense that God was saying, "Go to this basketball game."

He Inclined His Ear

Nancy received my leading without much question, especially when I told her I believed God was in it. She said, "If you believe that God is in this, then we ought to go."

We made the two hour trip to Winston Salem. At the basketball game, I spoke to only one other individual besides George Everding. That man was Matt Meinel, who was sitting on the bench behind George in the bleachers. I said to Matt, "Apparently you have a child playing here."

He said, "Yes, my son is on the same team as George's son."

Then I asked him what kind of work he did, and he said that he was in investment banking. "I just moved back after two years in London."

I said, "Oh that is very interesting, because I have been working for a period of time to create a financial services network to serve the global poor. It may be possible that your background in investment banking has some relationship with what I am doing."

He didn't tell me at the time, but days later when we talked again, he told me that the week before the basketball game, he had attended a meeting called the Half-Time Institute. A man named Bob Buford had set up this organization to give Christian people like Matt a chance to examine the course of their lives. Most of the people that attend the Half-Time Institute were very successful financially. They were asking themselves the question, now that they had "made it" and accumulated wealth in the world, what is it that they could do with their lives that would be for the glory of God. Matt explained to me that at that recent meeting, he had been challenged to write out a list of things that he might or could or should do.

At the top of his list was the phase, "I should use my international experience in banking to create a global financial services network to serve the rural poor."

When he met me at the basketball game and learned of my intentions, he had a strong understanding that we were there by God's appointment, that God had led us to each other. Out of that meeting came the international organization Wel-Fi. Wel-Fi is the result of years of thinking, planning, wondering and hoping.

W. Stephen Keel

For 12 years, Matt had been a former managing director in charge of purchasing technology for UBS, the largest investment banking company in the world. He agreed to be on our Wel-Fi board of directors. One of the things that he did, as director, was make a contact with the CFI of World Vision. He was able to do that because of his stature in the community of finance and his experience in this kind of activity.

The question has been asked, "How could Matt Meinel and Stephen Keel plan the evolution of mutually complementary goals and then arrange to meet each other?"

I have to conclude that it wasn't possible for us to do that. Our meeting was in fact part of what I refer to as the "divine choreography of God in the dance of life." God knew all about Matt, and He knew all about me. He knew all about what each of us was doing, and He made a decision on that particular night in the spring of 2007 to cause us to sit down next to each other at a basketball game. He caused us to realize that we both had been led by the Spirit of God to a future that was yet to be fully revealed.

The story about Wel-Fi and details about what I want to accomplish through it is not completely written at this moment. In fact in the past few days, my connections in Mexico have unraveled, and I have no clear idea what is going to happen next. In faith, I expect much but demand little. I am merely a love slave of Jesus, enjoying His presence and waiting to see what He wants to do next. He is a wonderful Savior, and I often wonder what in the world is going to happen next.

Let's go back to the beginning of the chapter. How could a fight with a computer and a prayer have any notable impact on me, or anybody else? I can trace the existence of Wel-Fi and Help for the Hungry to a fight with a computer. I heard the still small voice saying "Build chicken coops." I hope you can see this as clearly as I see it. I am postulating that hearing the voice of God is normal. I say this in light of the fact that many people think that it is "abnormal". Yes, it could appear "abnormal" because sometimes it has abnormal consequences, but God doesn't speak just to speak. He speaks because He has significant purposes in mind. The whole earth will be filled with His glory, as the waters cover the sea.

Chapter 14: Addendum

I don't know if the following stories relate to "hearing God's voice," but it occurs to me that there is value in recording them because this book is also a memoir. These things are interesting components of the life God gave to my wife and me. Some occurred before we came to know the Lord. We entered into marriage with a sense of eagerness for the wonderful life we wanted to live. The night we discussed our agreement to be wed, we also discussed traveling to Alaska and getting jobs as school teachers. We looked forward to the joys and adventures that people have when they are willing to take a little risk and go outside of the normal boundaries of living.

We spent our first years in Alaska. We were drawn into a situation where we had enough financial resources to purchase a small airplane. We used it as transportation to travel about the countryside. It was exciting and intimate. We didn't own much more than an airplane, a cat and a tent. We flew about, many times sleeping in the tent under the wing of the airplane.

One particular summer, we were in Fairbanks, Alaska in a tourist place called Alaska Land. It was created to celebrate the centennial purchase of Alaska. Many tourists came to visit in the summers. While we were there we had a small cabin at "Alaska Land" to live in. We didn't pay rent for the cabin because the program wasn't as successful as they had hoped. There was more display space than vendors. We set up a little shop selling smoked salmon from the Eskimos. I would fly up to a village on the Yukon River north of the Arctic Circle, purchase the smoked salmon and bring it back to sell to the tourists.

We also offered airplane rides to people and had some interesting events to occur while we were there. During this two-year period of our lives, we had five forced landings while flying airplanes: mechanical failures, failures in judgment, and weather problems. Any of them could have resulted in a fatal accident, but five times we successfully put the airplane down on the ground without damage.

God protected and prepared us for this life in Christ that was on the horizon. It is also interesting to note that in Alaska Land, we entered into a relationship with a man who was a pathological liar. At 23 years of age, this was my first experience of this kind. I didn't know that it was possible for anybody to live in so much denial of the truth that they would actually convince everyone around them of many untrue stories of wealth and adventure.

In this particular instance, a young man just slightly older than us let it be known that he was very wealthy. He owned two airplanes, gold mines, and he was knowledgeable about the gold market. He punctuated his stories by pulling nuggets of gold out of his pocket from a little pouch as we shared drinks in the "saloon" at Alaska Land. He appeared to be woodsy with a beard, but was he on the "up and up" with us? We had a friendship with him for several weeks and never suspected his duplicity. I had my first suspicion of the fault in his character when I took him on an airplane ride. He said his two planes were in the shop in Anchorage being worked on, so we couldn't see them.

We flew north over the White Mountains toward Circle, Alaska where he showed us his gold mine from the air. I couldn't distinguish anything on the ground other than forest and hills. We circled around an area several times, and he kept saying, "There is it right there! Get a little closer. That's it, right there!"

It was like the emperor with no clothes. I couldn't see anything at all, but he assured us that that was it. That was my first suspicion of something strange about him. As we headed back toward Fairbanks in good weather, I saw some sizable clouds along the way. I chose to fly through one of the clouds. That was not a legal maneuver and definitely not a wise thing to do in the "lower 48" states, but I was in the wilderness where the likelihood of there being another plane around was almost non-existent. I would be in the cloud for only a matter of seconds. As I flew into the cloud, I noticed the man trembling. He clenched his fist until the knuckles were white, and beads of sweat appeared on his forehead.

At that moment I knew that his stories about flying airplanes were a hoax. I didn't say anything, but we landed the airplane, and two days

He Inclined His Ear

later he had disappeared. It turned out he had been lying to many others as well and had borrowed money from many of them without repaying them. We were very thankful he hadn't asked us for money; the affair was a wake-up call. We gained insight and understanding into the nature and character of mankind.

Not too many years in the future, when we were in a church situation, we were able to discern and expose a pastor who was also a pathological liar. This isn't something I would promote, but the fact is that our experiences as non-Christians translated into a benefit to us later because we were protected from the many lies of an individual who was able to deceive many Christians. I am not sure how this fits into my story except to say that the hand of God is on our lives when we are saved and when we are unsaved. He is very interested in teaching us and molding us for His purposes. This small story is part of the manner in which the Lord trained us for His purposes.

Not only did He train us, He protected us. I have already mentioned five forced landings. I needed to know that life was not a mere matter of observation, but that it was indeed frail and fleeting.

The Lord purposed on a particular weekend while we were teaching school at Sand Point on the Aleutian Chain to show me an astounding coincidence, that now many years later I can say the hand of God functioned in my life. At the time I thought it was only coincidence. Like many who can't see how God inclines His ear unto us, I dismissed the coincidences at the time as being serendipitous.

I had an opportunity to go bear hunting one weekend with a fish and game biologist who worked for the State of Alaska. We had been dropped off by some fishermen on the mainland of the Alaskan peninsula in a totally uninhabited area. Sand Point was about 30 miles away on an island in the North Pacific. Gracious men in the community had given us a ride on their commercial fishing boat. They loaned us a small boat because the bay we entered didn't have a dock. We used their 16 foot skiff with a 50 horse power motor for the weekend. When we came to shore we looked for signs of animals and shot a couple of caribou. We used them for bear bait unsuccessfully.

We ate some of the caribou. Then next day we used the small boat to tour the bay. We hit a rock and sheered the cotter-key that enables the blade on the motor to turn. We hadn't anticipated this kind of mechanical difficulty, and we didn't have adequate tools to fix it. In a wilderness situation like this, one has to use his ingenuity. We did. We found a 16 penny nail partially driven into the side of the boat. We worked it loose and effectively made our own cotter-key to get the propeller going on the motor.

If we had not been able to do that, we would have been drifting about in a large bay in a totally uninhabited wilderness area, but we were successful. We drove the boat to shore. The biologist said he was interested in the flora and fauna of this area, and suggested that I hike over to the next bay to look for bears. We made the decision to split up. Around 9 p.m. I began a 12 mile hike to an adjacent bay along the Alaskan peninsula. The plan was to have the fishing boat pick him up first and then come over to the next bay to pick me up. There was a deserted cabin there I could stay in.

It was an invigorating time in the spring of the year. The weather was still cold. I came to a stream that flowed out of the mountains. It was too deep for me to cross due to high tide. I had with me, as everyone had in that community, a tide book. From it, I knew that in a few hours the tide would ebb enough that I could probably cross the stream. Since it was midnight now, I decided to lie down on the beach and get some rest. I had a plastic bag with caribou meat for something to eat and for bear bait on the hunting trip. I tried to sleep but I couldn't. My body was aching and sore from the strenuous hike. The brief darkness of the night lasted only three hours because of how far north Alaska is. I looked at the sky and the stars. It was an awesome experience lying there all alone. Finally, I slept for no more than 45 minutes.

When I awoke, the scheduled ebb of the tide had occurred, and I could now cross it. When I sat up, I looked at the sand and saw bear tracks only five feet from where I had been sleeping with the fresh caribou meat right next to me. These bear tracks indicated to me that it was an extremely large Alaskan grizzly bear. I had conflicting responses to this:

"I'm going to get a chance to shoot a big bear," or "Phew! That was a close call!"

He Inclined His Ear

Later the biologist explained to me that the bear had just come out of hibernation and was interested in kelp for cleansing its digestive system. That is likely why he was not attracted to me or the caribou meat. How fortunate for me; perhaps God protected me.

I waded across the stream going in the same direction as the bear had gone and tracked it for a mile. Then the tracks headed into some dense willows. I could either follow the bear or make a left hand turn along the trail to go to a cabin where I would sleep that night. I considered the situation: the willows were so thick that I couldn't see more than 10 feet ahead, so I decided I'd let this bear live, that I might live.

I went to the cabin, built a fire, and cooked a great supper of caribou meat, potatoes and baked beans. The cabin was already stocked with canned food. I went to sleep and awoke the next day to a howling, raging snow storm. About 10 inches of snow had fallen and the waves in the bay were significant. Having grown up in central New York State, I was accustomed to violent weather, and was largely comfortable and enjoying myself.

My wife wasn't enjoying herself back on the island. Seeing the violent storm, she had decided to come with the fishermen to pick us up. She made the 30 mile trip across the North Pacific in the midst of the blinding snow, howling winds and huge waves with a small crew of drunken fishermen. When they arrived at the first bay, the fish and game biologist came by himself out to the boat in the skiff. My wife and the fishermen saw that I wasn't with him. In this kind of climate, it was not uncommon for people to die. Three people had died that year in unusual sea accidents. The skiff took at least 15 minutes to come from shore to the boat, and all that time she and the fishermen thought something had happened to me. The drunks very timidly decided to go inside the boat cabin and leave my wife outside by herself to find out what had happened to me.

As the biologist pulled up, motor roaring, she could not talk to him until he cut the motor off. He had a smile on his face. Nancy did not have a smile on her face. She said, "Where is Steve?"

He said, "Oh, he went by himself over to the next bay yesterday. He didn't have any luck finding bear here so he should be about 12 miles over in the next lagoon."

She was comforted that there was no bad news, but it wasn't that comforting to realize that I had taken off trekking 12 miles alone in the wilderness, and now she had to continue in the middle of a blinding snow storm across the North Pacific Ocean to find out if I had made it okay. Well, I had and they did. They piloted the commercial fishing boat 12 more miles in the storm and anchored about a mile off shore.

I heard the sounds of the boat through the sounds of the storm from the cabin so I went outside and waved, and they waved back. The biologist got in the skiff and came to shore to pick me up. There was a very strong onshore wind with good size breakers on the beach, but by being cautious and counting the breakers, he found the seventh one which was the lowest one. I succeeded in jumping into the skiff and heading back out to the fishing boat. At the boat the swells were five to seven feet high. The only way we could get from the skiff to the fishing boat was to pull alongside. As the swells ebbed and flowed, the larger boat would go down and the skiff would go up. At a particular point, when the two boats were at virtually the same level, we stepped from one to the other. Then, we looked back and the skiff was seven feet below the fishing boat. Timing was everything in order to survive the North Pacific's frigid waters.

We tied off the skiff to the fishing boat and made the five-hour trek through the storm to the village of Sand Point. Nothing so far seemed to be out of the ordinary. What struck me as significant happened when we returned. When we got back to the safe harbor and out of the storm, I got into the skiff to return it to its owner. I pulled the starter cord on the engine and put it in gear, only to discover that the nail we used for a cotter pin had failed. The propeller was unable to spin. Instantly I recognized how serendipitous our return to the boat had been. Had the failure occurred during my return from the cabin in the swells of the sea, I could not have reached the boat due to the strong onshore wind. Those on the fishing boat would not have known what my problem was because I did not have a two-way radio.

He Inclined His Ear

The fishing boat would have had to return to Sand Point, a round trip of 60 miles, to get another skiff and come back for me at a later time.

All in all, it could have been a difficult situation, but trouble was averted by the fact that the cotter key held up until the moment I tried to return the boat. This example of "coincidence," I know now, was in preparation for a series of many more "coincidences" that I am relating to you in these memoirs. I also can say that I am confident that the hand of God was present in everything that occurred, even though I had not yet bowed my knee to the Lordship of Jesus Christ.

Chapter 15: Other Stories

Editor's note: The original manuscript for this book was completed in 2008. More events occurred in the subsequent years that can only be captured from Steve's emails.

August 2010: A Real Challenge

Some of you were aware of the fact that I had a doctor's appointment Thursday. The results were challenging.

My pulmonary function test indicated that my lungs are working at 57% of the capacity expected for a person my age, weight and height. The ability of my lungs to disperse oxygen into my bloodstream is 37% of normal. The CT scan clearly revealed some lung scarring, and the doctor said definitively that I have Idiopathic Pulmonary Fibrosis (IPF). There is no known cure for this condition. The best life expectancy is 6 years.

The disease is known to take one of 3 courses; rapid progress results in death in 18 months; slow progress yields 5-6 years of life expectancy with increasingly worse health; the third course is slow progress converting to rapid progress at any time.

My sister, Karen has IPF, so there is the suggestion that this condition is genetically induced. I will be taking part in a field trial that studies this issue. Our family members should be interested in this study to discover any personal risk. Karen is on a list for a lung transplant. The doctor will discuss a lung transplant with me when I see him on my birthday in December. A lung transplant can add 4-6 years of life once you get over the 1st year's difficulties with your body's ability to accept the lung.

Yes, all of this is challenging. Even so, the doctor cannot explain how my health improved so dramatically after being as sick as I was 11 months ago. Most days I feel pretty normal until I exert myself physically. When I do, my oxygen levels drop, and I have to slow down. I recover quite rapidly. The scar on my arm from the shop fire continues to improve dramatically. Our efforts to clean the house to reduce the impact of allergens have met with stunning success. I breathe

He Inclined His Ear

quite normally at night. The enzyme that I attribute to healing my scarred arm is Serrapeptase. My Duke doctor at never heard of it.

I am meeting this challenge using the comforts found in Psalm 116 and the health that I see in my life that is not supposed to be there. I had two other doctors tell me that they had never seen anyone with IPF recover from the depth sickness that I experienced.

This recent trip to the doctor will be a benchmark. In December, I will have either held my ground, improved or see evidence of decay. In the meantime, the challenge is to do what I do and to treat every day as a precious gift. I intend to travel and exercise as my health allows.

This description of the problem is fairly cryptic. I am not in denial, yet I cannot deny the health I have experienced either. Many fine saints have prayed for me over the last two years. I am sure the Lord will expand my spirit understanding significantly in the months to come. Until you have the kind of conversation with a physician, like the one we had Thursday, Psalm 116 does not have quite the fullness that I now see in it. Here it is for your edification…

I love the LORD because He hears my voice and my prayer for mercy.

Because He bends down to listen, I will pray as long as I have breath!

Death wrapped its ropes around me; the terrors of the grave overtook me. I saw only trouble and sorrow.

Then I called on the name of the LORD: "Please, LORD, save me!"

How kind the LORD is! How good He is! So merciful, this God of ours!

The LORD protects those of childlike faith; I was facing death, and He saved me.

Let my soul be at rest again, for the LORD has been good to me.

He has saved me from death, my eyes from tears, my feet from stumbling.

And so I walk in the LORD's presence as I live here on earth!

I believed in You, so I said, "I am deeply troubled, LORD."

W. Stephen Keel

In my anxiety I cried out to You, "These people are all liars!"

What can I offer the LORD for all He has done for me?

I will lift up the cup of salvation and praise the LORD's name for saving me.

I will keep my promises to the LORD in the presence of all His people.

The LORD cares deeply when His loved ones die.

O LORD, I am Your servant; yes, I am Your servant, born into Your household; You have freed me from my chains.

I will offer You a sacrifice of thanksgiving and call on the name of the LORD.

I will fulfill my vows to the LORD in the presence of all His people— in the house of the LORD in the heart of Jerusalem.

Praise the LORD!

(Psalm 116:1-19)

Resting in Him,

W. Stephen Keel

March 2011: Another day in the life of Steve aka Dad Keel.

Riding in a race car at the Virginia International Raceway (VIR)

120 M.P.H. on a 1/4 mile straight stretch followed by a series of S curves descending with a 12 degree slope....that can cause you to wonder just when is a good time to hit the brakes in preparation for the curve. The Bimmer decelerates remarkably well. After another short flat-out run, I learned that "losing your grip" on the pavement in a curve is SOP and can give you a 12% speed bump as long as you regain your grip in time to continue around the track.

So, Marguerite, why is it that the macho guys don't have hair?

The real challenge was fitting the helmet over my head with the oxygen tubes over my ears. Those helmets are a bit stuffy due to the restricted air flow. I had to turn the air flow up to 5 lpm. Ears bent

He Inclined His Ear

backwards in a tight helmet are hard enough to straighten out, even without the oxygen tubes.

Getting in and out between the roll bars is pretty easy for a 19-year-old, like the kid with the new Porsche who was getting driving lessons from Than. He is the kid who literally jumps through the window feet first. It took two guys to pull me out after the parade lap. The exercise-induced asthma attack that followed let the drivers know that I was not in top shape. The second time, in and out of the car, I did better, except the second time was when we did the high speed run. I nearly fainted when I first stood outside the car, but that passed pretty quickly, and I found a lawn chair near the network security manager for Brookhaven Laboratories on Long Island. I was able to describe my trip to their lab years ago when I was measuring boundary-layer winds for environmental studies with a kite on a 2000 foot Kevlar line.

The sideways motion in the curves never exceeded 2 G's, so I was pretty comfortable as long as I stopped pushing my feet against the cramped floor board and allowed my body to totally relax in the tight-fitting chair and body harness.

Than, an experienced instructor, was careful to note my comfort level on the first few laps before taking the Bimmer closer to competition speeds. I had already regaled him with some of my flying escapades, so he wasn't too concerned about my capacity for riding on the edge.

Nathaniel nicknamed "Than" is rolling out a $15 million software install for Citi Corp in 100 countries. He mentioned that there are not too many people qualified for his job. He travels internationally 3 or 4 times a year, teaching race driving from March to September and racing cars himself in October.

Than is a guest this weekend at one of the houses we advertise at Staynearby.com. I happened to chat with him on the phone about a deposit check and mentioned that my appetite for speed had been taken care of when I was a bush pilot in Alaska. He responded by asking me if I would like to ride the track at VIR with him. This particular day at the track was scheduled for racing students that pay big bucks for lessons, but he, as an instructor, had the liberty to offer me a ride and I jumped at it.

I spent 6 hours at the track. I spent several minutes riding in a golf cart to the men's room, hobnobbing with a guy that has a 45 million dollar air conditioning business in Alabama and who, the night before, had beat out 59 cars in a 13-hour endurance race that ended at 1am. Twenty-five of the cars broke down from the stress and did not finish the race. There was more than one driver per car. Two hours at a stretch is enough to fray the nerves of most. I watched the guy that won the race pay an additional $95 to score a few more relaxing laps around the course, a mere 12 hours after the race ended.

Sick as I am, being confined to 24-hour oxygen and plagued with heavy coughing fits every day or two, I am still me, and I guess the Lord wanted me to have one more thrilling experience. (As much fun as it was, it did not compare to driving a "wind-up" minivan through the neighborhoods of Bogotá, Columbia, or with taking my wife to a beach in El Salvador to watch me get caught a rip tide in the Pacific Ocean.) Just minutes prior to this incident, I had read her a Psalm about being rescued from danger by the Lord. Funny thing, the rip tide did not get me.

Not much is happening here in boring Pittsylvania County. That's why you all moved away, isn't it? Hope you enjoyed my reflections on the day.

Love, Dad

November 2011: Stephen Keel - New Lung Needed - Monday 11/28 Update

The reports of my early demise are greatly exaggerated. Yes, I have a fatal disease that could take me soon without intervention. Intervention is at hand.

A lung transplant appears to be close...8-20 days out. In the meantime, I refer to myself as the healthiest sick person in the hospital (day 8). I am a one-health issue guy. My lungs are failing, but the rest of me is really pretty healthy. I am totally dependent on oxygen. There is a small chance that I could leave the hospital to wait for a lung, but that is uncertain.

He Inclined His Ear

I am working several hours a day in my new office at Duke University Hospital. I can talk on the phone (919 681-7823) and write emails.

The single-lung transplant surgery and recovery are intense; 12-16 hours on the table, no food for several days or weeks afterward, and about 16 weeks in the hospital, depending on complications which are common. I have no idea how long it will be until I am able to use the computer after the surgery, so I am working hard to get Mobile Evangelism activities underway or reported on prior to the surgery.

My physical condition prior to the surgery has a profound effect on the number of complications I will experience. 15 laps around the hall measures one mile. I have been doing 3 miles a day with substantial amounts of oxygen. I hope to walk 4 or 5 miles a day soon.

Take meds

Walk

Talk to doctor

Write emails

Walk

Take meds

Talk on phone

Write emails

Ride wheelchair to cafeteria and sidewalk outside of the hospital

Walk

Take Meds

Repeat as needed and be ready psychologically and spiritually for surgery.

So what am I learning from all of this?

Living for others is the most rewarding way to live. Whether you are caring for your small children, nursing your sick husband, delivering a meal to a friend or distributing gospel literature to cell phones globally, the fact that you are living for others is the best motivation for continuing to live. I am highly motivated to undergo the rigors of the

W. Stephen Keel

surgery because I have meaning and purpose in my life. I believe that I have made a difference in the lives of others and that the Lord is going to continue to use me. I have been walking and listening to John Michael Talbot's song "Make Me an Instrument of Your Peace."

My friend, George Everding, spent the night with me last night. We discussed the fact that I have already received instances of creative restoration of body parts. I also have a revelation of the fact that God loves the world so much that He has placed scientific knowledge in the hands of men so that His hand could be extended to people with and without faith; think "grace and mercy" at the hospital. I prefer the creative healing and am asking for it, but I will not despise the help from a person's family who loses a loved one that I might have a lung.

Although I realize that good friends object to my standing on promises from the Old Testament, here is what I have received. (Please note, I learned a long time ago to "give no place to the devil.")

Not all affliction is punishment.

Sickness does not necessarily mean sinfulness.

Jesus Heals a Man Born Blind

[1]As Jesus was walking along, he saw a man who had been blind from birth. [2]"Rabbi," his disciples asked him, "why was this man born blind? Was it because of his own sins or his parents' sins?"

[3]"It was not because of his sins or his parents' sins," Jesus answered. "This happened so the power of God could be seen in him. [4]We must quickly carry out the tasks assigned us by the one who sent us. The night is coming, and then no one can work. [5]But while I am here in the world, I am the light of the world."

Think http://www.kioskevangelism.com.

(Psa 119:67) *"Before I was afflicted I went astray: but now have I kept thy word."*

(Psa 119:71) *"It is good for me that I have been afflicted; that I might learn thy statutes."*

(Psa 119:75) *"I know, O LORD, that thy judgments are right, and that thou in faithfulness hast afflicted me."*

He Inclined His Ear

Psalm 119:73-77

⁷³Your hands have made me and fashioned me;

Give me understanding, that I may learn Your commandments.

⁷⁴Those who fear You will be glad when they see me,

Because I have hoped in Your word.

⁷⁵I know, O LORD, that Your judgments are right,
And that in faithfulness You have afflicted me.

⁷⁶Let, I pray, Your merciful kindness be for my comfort,
According to Your word to Your servant.

⁷⁷Let Your tender mercies come to me, that I may live;
For Your law is my delight.

Affliction brought the psalmist to focus on his relationship with God, and His Word. Rather than feeling sorry for himself, he realized how blessed he was to know God and to rest upon His promises.

What about us today? Where are we at in our relationship with our Lord?

Do the trials and tribulations move us away from our faith, or do they reaffirm where we stand?

Finally, I am resting in the precious promises in James, Chapter 1... Count it all joy, my brethren, when ye fall into manifold trials/tests/temptations; Knowing that the proving of your faith worketh patience. And let patience have its perfect work, that ye may be perfect and entire, lacking in nothing.

"Lacking nothing" sounds like the abundant life to me. Pressure creates diamonds. I hope to shine even brighter very soon.

In Christ,

W. Stephen Keel

October 2012: Plans for Steve's Celebration

Dear Friends and Family,

I am sad and happy to inform you that Steve went home to be with the Lord last night about 6 p.m. He had all of his children around him singing for the last several hours of his life. He was awake and aware some of the time and even wrote a couple of notes. He had suffered untold misery and pain recently and also much of the time during the last 10 months at Duke University hospital. As you remember, he had two separate lung transplants last winter. He never recovered from the second lung transplant.

The family plans to celebrate his life at home at 11a.m. on Friday. Friends and family are invited to come at that time or whenever they wish to stop by. A potluck meal will be held at home as part of the celebration.

God is sustaining me through this time of Steve's departure. Psalm 34 has been a recurring theme for strength for me. I am not perplexed as to why Steve's time was sooner than we expected, but I am finding continued answers each day in His Word. Your prayers have been felt and much appreciated in these past few days by me and the kids.

His peace and grace have been more than sufficient for me.

In Him,

Nancy at Steve's computer

W. Stephen Keel

Epilogue

For we are His workmanship, created in Christ Jesus for good works, which God prepared beforehand that we should walk in them.
Ephesians 2:10

One afternoon in late September 2012, as we sat around Dad's bed in the Duke University Hospital room 7813, we reflected upon the goodness of God in Dad's life. Sunlight streamed from the single window on to the end of the bed. Mom stood near the top of the bed, leaning against the frame. I perched on the edge at the end of the bed. Several other siblings were there. It was not a sad time. We had now spent nine months with Dad at the Duke University Hospital, and we were very accustomed to afternoons like these. I knew at the time that those few moments were yet another snapshot in time, like so many of the stories in this book. We had just finished reading the "Addendum" chapter of this book. We marveled at the amazing life Dad had led to that point, how the Lord had choreographed his life, from the redemption on the shoreline of Alaska, to his dramatic salvation, to the culmination of his work with mobile evangelism. From the time of his salvation, Dad firmly believed in the promise that he was "created for good works, that God prepared beforehand." He steadfastly sought to follow the Lord and "walk in them."

Dad pursued the work the Lord had prepared for him until the very end. Several weeks prior, Dad had been readmitted to the hospital because of simple aspiration. With his new lungs, he could not feel the aspiration, but within a matter of hours, the increased need for oxygen forced him to check back into the hospital after only being out for a few weeks. Dad knew if he went back, he might never get out of the hospital again. That Saturday, after he was established again as a patient at Duke, Chris and I visited him. He needed company on his first night back. The hospital food did not appeal to Dad, so we all went down to the cafeteria to dine on chicken fingers. The late August day was cool enough to enjoy dinner outside on the cafeteria patio.

He Inclined His Ear

We spent the bulk of the meal discussing Dad's work with mobile evangelism.

"I am transferring all my work on mobile evangelism to a guy in Atlanta. He is fully prepared to take on the ministry and continue to promote it. I spoke with him the other day," Dad explained to us.

I couldn't understand why Dad was giving up the ministry he had pursued for the last three years. In his first days at the hospital, he had set up his office in his hospital room. While hooked to oxygen, he took phone calls from around the world to discuss mobile evangelism.

"But you will be out again soon and can continue this work?" I responded.

"No, Clyde is much better positioned to run it at this point. He has the energy, understanding, and vision to move it forward."

The inevitability of it all was tough. I didn't want Dad to give his ministry away. I firmly believed the new lungs were an answer to prayer and would allow Dad to continue promoting the mobile evangelism ministry. But here was Dad, actually excited at the prospect that someone else would promote it. Nancy Stephanie later told me that some years prior Dad had had a dream. In the dream God allowed him to start something big, but Dad would not be around to see it come to fruition.

In March 2009, Dad and Mom took a three-week trip to India. The trip was at the invitation of Pastor Samuel Prasad. Dad had happened to meet Samuel at a Christian summer camp in Virginia a year prior. Much like the stories in this book, the encounter was a divine appointment. Samuel spent many weeks with Dad on Keel Hill, and later he invited him to preach in his churches in India.

While in India, Dad noticed that even the poorest of the poor had cell phones. He was particularly struck by a man standing in a rice field talking on his cell phone. Dad's work with Wel-Fi and mobile banking had already opened his eyes to the proliferation of cellphones around the world. At that moment he was inspired! What if we could get the Word of God on that man's cellphone and anyone else's cellphone in the remotest parts of the world? Dad returned home with a determination to reach the multitudes for Christ through the cell phone technology.

Like everything else in his life, Dad fully engaged in mobile evangelism. Sixty percent of the world population cannot read. These people can only receive the Word of God by listening to someone read it. Almost all cell phones have an audio playing device. Dad started by figuring how to get free audio Christian materials for cellphone. Also, because cellphone services are so expensive, many buy minutes on cards. So Dad investigated how to get the Christian materials on a phone for free, either through downloading from Micro SD cards or Bluetooth.

Dad started testing the concept immediately. He worked with indigenous pastors in Colombia, Mexico, and India. He also tested at Coicom, the Spanish Christian Broadcasters Association at the annual meeting in the Dominican Republic in 2009. Long lines of people waited for him to download Bibles, Christian teachings, and music onto their cellphones. The concept proved to be a resounding success.

Dad knew this concept was bigger than anything he had done before. After the Coicom experience, Dad contacted a number of large major Christian ministries and explained to them his ideas and experiences with the cell phone. They began to catch the vision. It is like the invention of an audio Gutenberg Press, the Bible can now be freely given to anyone who has a cell phone.

In December 2010, Dad hosted the first annual meeting of Christian organizations called Mobile Ministry Forum on Keel Hill. Twelve men representing different missionary organizations gathered to discuss mobile evangelism. The purpose of the forum was to discuss the current strategies of how to get the audio Gospel onto cell phones in closed and remote areas. Today the Mobile Ministry Forum (http://www.mobileministryforum.org) is a vibrant network of ministry organizations working together to use mobile technology for the advance of the Good News of Jesus Christ. The Forum has gathered many times since that initial meeting in the United States and around the world.

He Inclined His Ear

The End of the Beginning

For I know that my Redeemer lives, And He shall stand at last on the earth; And after my skin is destroyed, this I know, That in my flesh I shall see God. Job 19:25-26

Dad stepped out of this life into eternity with the Giver of Life on October 9, 2012. He was surrounded by his wife, all his children, some son-in-laws, grandchildren, Ruffin and Jamie Shackelford, and George Everding. We were crammed in that same 7813 room at Duke University Hospital. God's grace was sufficient to allow us to celebrate with Dad. We sang and worshiped for several hours that afternoon as we waited for Jesus to receive Dad.

Two days prior the doctors had decided that the recent injury to the lungs was irreversible, and Dad could not recover. For the last nine months we had firmly believed, prayed, fasted, and anointed Dad in the belief that he would be healed. He had been healed so many times prior in his life. Only a week prior we held a prayer meeting for healing and believed like the prophet Ezekiel that God would breathe life into the dry bones. But God's ways are not our ways, and Dad's ordained time had come. We had jointly agreed to move Dad to palliative care and to remove the ventilator that afternoon.

The last two months of Dad's life were not easy. The physical and spiritual anguish of the lung transplant and prolonged hospital stay took a toll on his sanity. His faith was challenged. I firmly believe his suffering is being rewarded in heaven. He knew his work was finished and he desired to go home to heaven. He had been unable to speak the last month because of the ventilator. When the doctors asked him how he felt those two days prior, he wrote "Expectant."

"So, I go off man's medication into the hands of God. At that time we will know the purpose of God," he wrote after our decision to end the Duke lung transplant program.

The purpose of God was revealed as we sang "Amazing Grace" around the hospital bed that afternoon. It was the end of the beginning for Dad.

I did not want Dad to go. I had expected another 10 to 15 years with him. I did not think it was fair for God to take him after He had used him in so many ways. Doesn't the book of Proverbs promise long life for the righteous?

George Everding called me a week before Dad passed to give me an update on his prognosis. George was a godsend to Dad and to the family. He spent many days and nights at the hospital with Dad. When family members were exhausted from hospital stays, George was always willing to stay with Dad.

He did not bring good news this time.

"The prognosis is not good. I don't think your father has very long to live."

I pushed back; Dad would get through this setback too.

George responded, "I read the story about Moses and Joshua this morning and reflected on it. Moses led the Israelites to the Promised Land, but while he saw the Promised Land, he was not allowed to enter it. Moses was the only prophet who spoke face-to-face with God. He heard from God. I feel like we are at that time with your Dad. God has led him to the brink of the Promised Land. Each one of you [his children] is a piece of your Dad. I have witnessed it so clearly in the last several months as I have gotten to know you. But like Moses, your Dad's time has come to an end. He cannot go forth any further, but each of you will go forth into the Promised Land and take hold of the promises of God. God led your Dad and your family to this point. Now it is time for you to move forward without him."

This was not an easy word to receive at the time, but it brought great comfort in the following weeks and months.

We are going forth. The Lord told Joshua in the first chapter of Joshua, "As I was with Moses, so I will be with you; I will never leave you nor forsake you." Then three times He commands him to be "strong and courageous."

Within weeks of Dad's passing, Mom spoke at Mobile Ministry Forum about Dad's life and ministry. Within months, she and Nancy Stephanie traveled to Kenya to work with pastors on mobile evangelism. In 2014, Mom, Marguerite, and Eric went to Coicom in Cali, Columbia to freely give again audio Bibles in all the Central and

He Inclined His Ear

South American languages to pastors to distribute via cell phone in their local churches. Chris and I have gone to India three times, including Marguerite on one trip, to minister to pastors. We brought with us audio New Testaments in Telugu on Micro SD cards to hand to them, just as Dad would have done.

God ignited in Mom the passion to search and catalog all the known free audio Bibles online. For six months she cataloged audio Bibles in 100's of languages. She gave away Micro SD cards, flash drives, and external hard drives loaded with Bibles and Christian material to any missionary who asked (even those who didn't know to ask).

Thus BibleTransmission was born. BibleTransmission is currently the only website that links the world to all of the known free online audio Bibles or portion of Bibles. The website is a product of Mom and all the Keel children.

God's ways are not our ways. We may plan our path, but God directs our steps (Proverbs 16). This book is not an easy read, especially for those who believe salvation is all about redemption from hell and an eternity in heaven when we get to walk with God. God is active in our daily lives, whether we wish to acknowledge it or not. When we do, we can see His divine chorography.

Dad wrote this book in 2008 as a legacy to his family. Since his passing I felt the urging to formally publish the draft manuscript. While my Dad is one of the most fascinating people I know, the purpose of this book is not to promote him, but to bring all glory to God. And, to encourage everyone that the God of the universe desires an intimate, personal relationship with us.

Rebecca Keel Ayers

W. Stephen Keel
Be Strong and Courageous

Since the loss of Steve, (that is what I call him when the children aren't present.) I have sought God with continual intensity as I did when he was so sick in the hospital. I put my whole heart into God's Word because it gave me hope and strength in those gut-wrenching days. I have not lost that "ground" of great intimacy with God. I often rise at 4 a.m. and pray or sit for two hours in the mornings lost in the presence of the Holy Spirit showing me many delightful things in Scripture.

Steve and I had asked God for abundance years ago. What we meant was that we did not want to limit God in what he wanted to do for us and through us. That principle is still with me today. The abundance of those years included an abundance of poverty and abundance of wealth, abundance of children and abundance of ministry, the abundance of joy and abundance of trials. I had not thought of abundance of trials until Steve became sick. The Scripture that we liked to overlook became a reality, "the fellowship of His suffering being made conformable unto his death, if by any means I might attain unto the resurrection of the dead." (Philippians 3:10-11) "Looking to Jesus the author and finisher of our faith; who for the joy that was set before him endured the cross, despising the shame, and is set down at the right hand of the throne of God." (Hebrews 12:2)

Steve understood that the Gospel would reach the ends of the earth through mobile evangelism very soon. He dropped producing his radio programs "A Proverb A Day" (which were playing on 300+ radio stations in 26 countries) to devote full time to mobile evangelism. Mobile phones will soon surpass radio and every other form of mass communication. He knew from experience that distant and remote people eagerly wanted Christian materials. He considered the use of hot spots and kiosks that would dispense free digital Gospel in malls, train stations, or any public place. He took many ideas and tested them several times "in the field." They were resoundingly successful even five years ago. Steve was still thinking "sandals on the ground" and offline distribution directly to the people. But another BIG step was around the corner that he could only dream about.

He Inclined His Ear

As of 2015, mobile phones have penetrated well into the small villages of Africa, Asia, and South America. I have a practice of sitting in his office at his desk continuing his research, and contacting his associates and friends. I seem to have acquired his fertile mind so that I might take mobile evangelism to the next step. For me, this next step eclipses all that have preceded it. In his earlier efforts, we saw the immense effort it took to teach and equip Christians to take the Gospel by mobile to the foreign field. Many mission-minded saints were too busy or yawned at the idea. Even today only a few people visit BibleTransmission. In many ways it seems a loss of time and money without making any significant headway for the Kingdom of God.

In November of 2014, I received a novel idea. How could I bypass equipping evangelists and give the Gospel from Steve's desk straight to the mobiles in Africa? I consulted another ministry and asked them to recommend a mobile ad agency. Normally an ad agency would take someone's product and sell it to affluent people in developed nations. Could the poorer regions of the world be similarly reached? They would not have much money. Was the satellite and cell tower infrastructure in place? Much to my surprise, that infrastructure is very much in place the world over.

With Marguerite's help, we concocted an unusual idea. Why couldn't we buy advertising from a mobile ad agency to offer Gospel media directly to mobile in remote and developing regions? And, that is exactly what we did. I choose the country of Benin, Africa, a very tiny nation of five million on the African west coast. I used the Gospel stories where Jesus is performing miracles. After the landing page was created for mobile in French, I paid $60 at $5 a day for a non-static banner ad to be placed with an ad agency named BuzzCity. I did not seriously consider that Benin had only a 220,000 mobile "reach," so my ad overflowed to other places in the world.

Nevertheless, this test ad resulted in about four thousand clicks worldwide, with about one thousand clicks for Benin. Of about one thousand clicks for Benin, only six hundred clicks were "non-bounced." That meant that six hundred viewers actually clicked on the site. They spent an average of 3.3 minutes listening or downloading 3.28 pages. They were all located in Cotonou, Benin, a port city of 450,000 people. Google analytics and CrazyEgg were used to verify these statistics. The cost was 10 cents each ($60 divided by 600 bona fide visits). This is so much cheaper any other method we have tried to date. Interestingly, my banner ad was shown on adult and game websites. You know, Jesus was a friend of sinners!

I have contacted a number of large international mission organizations telling them about this ad campaign, and I have received some amazing commendations. As of the publishing of this book, 10 ad campaigns offering a free audio download of Gospel stories are scheduled to run in 10 countries in 10 languages: Indonesia, Tanzania, Brazil, Turkey, Vietnam, India, Mexico, China, Sudan, and Bangladesh. I anticipated thousands upon thousands of clicks for downloads and listening. I organized it and collected the data for all the campaigns at Steve's desk....a good feeling!

Additionally, a second idea that Steve would appreciate has been given to me from two other ministries. It is a method of using Facebook as the ad agency and Facebook members as the recipients of my ad. I can target a city in India and have them click to visit my webpage with a free Gospel media in their language.

I think that Steve would say to me, "Go, Nancy! Go as fast and as hard as you can. Time is short. I am so glad that you took up where I left off and have finished my vision of reaching the ends of the earth for Christ. When this task of remote evangelism is completed in the world, then the Lord will return, and we will be together again in heaven and never to be separated forever."

Nancy H. Keel

He Inclined His Ear

W. Stephen Keel

Life in Pictures

Steve's school portrait in 1957.

Steve and Nancy at their wedding in June 18, 1967.

Steve and Nancy in their Cessna 180 in 1969. They flew the airplane to Alaska and up and down the East Coast.

He Inclined His Ear

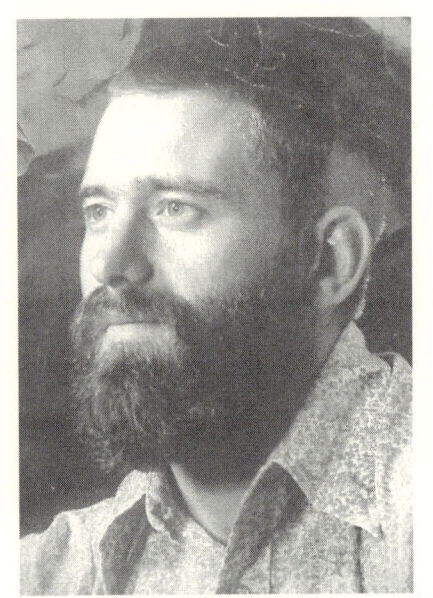

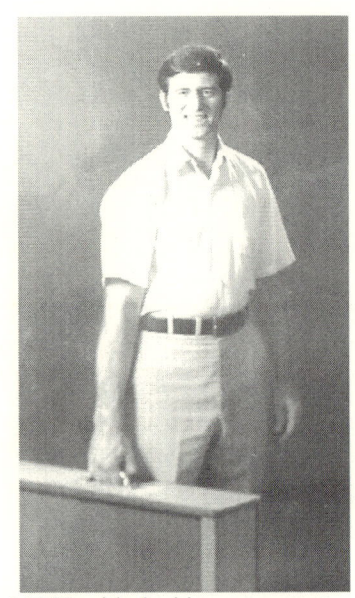

Steve right after becoming a Christian in 1973 and 1982 with the kite anemometer.

In the front yard in 1988. This picture was taken for his prison ministry newsletter.

W. Stephen Keel

Keel Family Portrait 1983. They had just returned to Virginia from New Mexico.

Steve and Nancy in 1993. Steve was continuing his prison ministry, but now owned National Computer Solutions in Danville, Virginia.

He Inclined His Ear

The Keel Family at Christmas 1997 with Steve's parents and Nancy's mother.

Nancy advertising one of the Henspas for the website. Steve started Egganic Industries in 1999. He successfully sold many models like this and other more deluxe models through 2009. The concept led to "Help for the Hungry" and 'Wel-Fi."

W. Stephen Keel

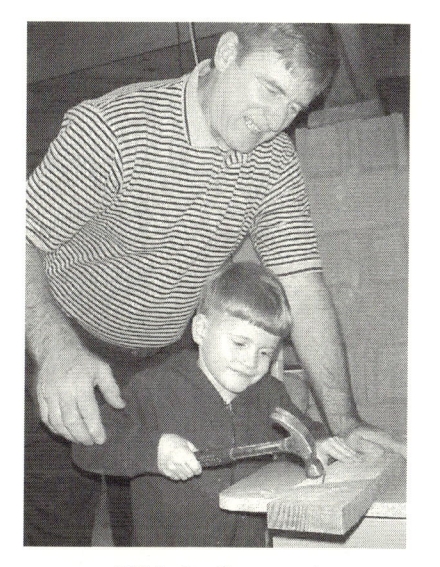

With the first grandson, Nathan DeVos in 2003 and again in 2007.

Recording "A Proverb A Day" from the home office.

He Inclined His Ear

In Haiti with Radio Lumiere and "A Proverb A Day" translator Lancy in 2003.

Advertising booth for "A Proverb A Day" at the Coicom Conference in El Salvador in 2006.

W. Stephen Keel

Demonstrating Kiosk Evangelism at the Coicom Conference in the Dominican Republic in 2008.

Listening to a presentation at the first Mobile Ministry Forum meeting at his home in December 2010.

He Inclined His Ear

Steve and Nancy in September 2011 at Nancy Stephanie's wedding.

Last family portrait with everyone at Nancy's and Jake's wedding September 2011. Left to right: Melissa Kreye, Jesse Kreye, Angie Cook, Rebecca Ayers, Chris Ayers, Marguerite Inscoe (holding Madeline), Eric Inscoe (holding Roman), Nancy Keeler, Jake Keeler, Nancy, Steve, Michelle Keel (holding Ella), Zeke Keel, David DeVos, Charissa Keel, Nathan DeVos, Rose of Sharon DeVos, Austin DeVos, and Sean DeVos.

W. Stephen Keel

Nancy speaking at the Mobile Ministry Forum in Orlando in December 2012. Steve's picture from the first Mobile Ministry Forum in 2010 is in the background.

Nancy sharing audio files with a pastor in Kenya in 2013.